MW01600903

A MOUNTAIN *of a* SERMON

KIM MATTHEWS

WESTBOW
PRESS®
A DIVISION OF THOMAS NELSON
& ZONDERVAN

Copyright © 2024 Kim Matthews.

All rights reserved. No part of this book may be used or reproduced by
any means, graphic, electronic, or mechanical, including photocopying,
recording, taping or by any information storage retrieval system
without the written permission of the author except in the case of
brief quotations embodied in critical articles and reviews.

WestBow Press books may be ordered through booksellers or by contacting:

WestBow Press
A Division of Thomas Nelson & Zondervan
1663 Liberty Drive
Bloomington, IN 47403
www.westbowpress.com
844-714-3454

Because of the dynamic nature of the Internet, any web addresses or
links contained in this book may have changed since publication and may
no longer be valid. The views expressed in this work are solely those
of the author and do not necessarily reflect the views of the publisher,
and the publisher hereby disclaims any responsibility for them.

Any people depicted in stock imagery provided by Getty Images are
models, and such images are being used for illustrative purposes only.
Certain stock imagery © Getty Images.

Unless otherwise indicated, scripture quotations are taken from the Holy Bible,
New International Version®, NIV®. Copyright © 1973, 1978, 1984 by Biblica,
Inc.™ Used by permission of Zondervan. All rights reserved worldwide.

Scripture quotations marked KJV are taken from
the Holy Bible, King James Version.

ISBN: 979-8-3850-1593-1 (sc)
ISBN: 979-8-3850-1594-8 (hc)
ISBN: 979-8-3850-1595-5 (e)

Library of Congress Control Number: 2023924628

Print information available on the last page.

WestBow Press rev. date: 5/6/2024

CONTENTS

DEDICATION

To Brenda, my amazing wife of fifty years
Thank you for your love and devotion. You are a blessing
to me. I also want to thank you for your dedication and
service to God. You have truly been an inspiration in
my life. Without God and you by my side, this project
would not have been possible. I love you always.

ACKNOWLEDGMENTS

First and foremost, I would like to thank God for His love, grace, and mercy. All things are possible through Him. I would like to show appreciation to my parents, Harold and Helena Matthews, for raising me to know the Lord and being true examples of faithful servants. I would like to thank my wife, children, and grandchildren for their love and patience while I worked on this project over the past thirty years. Thank you to my brothers and sisters in Christ who have supported me during my calling to bring His message to others. To my brothers from the Sunset School of Preaching, I am grateful for the continued bond we share as we lift each other up as inspired by His word. Thank you to my professors at Sunset School of Preaching for helping me gain a greater understanding of His teachings. To Professor Ted Kell, who first introduced me in depth to the Sermon on the Mount, I owe many thanks. I am humbled by your response to this project. It is a great honor to know that you would have used my project to teach the students at Sunset. To Jack Exum, for your support and suggestion in putting my project to print, I am extremely grateful.

INTRODUCTION

Now when he saw the crowds, he went up on a
mountainside and sat down. His disciples came
to him, and he began to teach them, saying ...
(Matthew 5:1–2)

The introduction to the Sermon on the Mount is very unpretentious
and innocent. The thought that these few words could lead to a
discourse of such a world-changing magnitude is remarkable.
The sermon is the backbone, the benchmark, the essence, or
any other descriptive term you choose to use, of the embodiment
of the teaching of the Lord of the universe. It does not contain
everything Jesus taught. It does not elaborate on some specifics
that we may crave in this information age. The sermon does give
simple information, but simple information is not His purpose.
The sermon is not just a compilation of mini-sermons. The
sermon embodies spiritual maturity, relationships, hints of the
divine nature, mirrors of the human condition, purpose, motives,
attitudes, warnings, faithfulness, a call to action, and more diverse
and thought-provoking concepts than I can fathom. The sermon
is the heart of God revealed to the hearts of men.

I could approach this text of Matthew 5–7 as a political fact-
finding mission that displays my preconceptions of years gone by.
Instead, I have chosen to try to take off my rose-colored glasses
of presupposition and look at this passage in a different way. This

venture has come from painful and painstaking self-assessment of both my motives and my presuppositions. It has been weighed and reweighed, counted, and recounted many more times than any of the presidential ballots. This journey into the sermon has taken me on a thirty-year odyssey through much study and more prayer. I hope it continually takes me on a journey for the rest of my years as well. So I offer it to you. This could prove to be helpful, or you may choose to dismiss it. It has given me the opportunity to let the plow down a little deeper. For that experience, I will be forever grateful to Jesus. I do not intend this to be simply a research mechanism. I have not included an abundance of quotes from many significant biblical scholars. That, I am sure, is a weakness. Yet many times, simple quotes are taken from the contexts of authors in a legalistic way to try and give credence to the concepts to be proposed. This is the one reason I have tried to refrain from quotes of supporting literature.

When I consider any biblical passage, there are certain things that I try to determine. Who is speaking? To whom is the passage spoken? What are the circumstances? Most of the time, the answers are obvious, as with the sermon. The speaker is Jesus. The disciples and the crowd are Jews following Christ. The circumstances are during the ministry of the Lord on earth. These elements, if consistently applied, are extremely helpful in the study of any passage and this is true of the sermon as well.

One thing I have tried to do in this book, which simple contextual hermeneutics does not address, is to look at the underlying principles that Jesus preached. By this I mean, there are certain principles that are the foundation of why Jesus made a particular statement. One way I can illustrate this proposal is found in the Ten Commandments. In Exodus 20:1–17, the Ten Commandments are listed. These commands are truly clear and deliver the intention of the Lord to Israel. These commands can be obeyed without any thought of the underlying principle behind the command. But if we look at the command, we can see the implied reason the command is given. The command "You shall not misuse the name of the Lord your God" implies by the nature of the command that the principle behind the command is "The Lord's name is holy." This command is given to ensure that the principle of the holiness of the Lord's name is maintained. "You shall not murder" is a very stern directive. Yet the principle behind the command implies that life is precious, and it is not to be terminated.

A preacher mentioned this concept in one of his sermons. In a passing comment, the preacher mentioned the idea of a principle behind a command. I do not remember the preacher's name; nor do I remember another thing about the preacher's sermon. The idea of the principle behind the command mentioned by that preacher caused my mind to wander during that sermon, and the wandering continues.

Another thing that has helped me in my understanding is a concept found in a little book by Mike Cope on the Sermon on the Mount titled *Righteousness Inside Out*.[1] In this book, Cope looks at several passages from the sermon and writes about how Jesus was trying to change folks from the heart out and not just regulate their actions. It is worth the read.

These two concepts have changed the entire way I approach scripture. For me, it eliminates the legalistic, lawyer-type parsing of passages that leads to self-righteousness for those who hold that position and leads to condemned consciences for those who do not. This has been a freedom expedition for me. To say it has set me on a grace-filled journey of indescribable joy is an epic understatement. It has helped me beyond words.

---

[1] Mike Cope, *Righteousness Inside Out* (Nashville, Tennessee, Christian Communications, A division of the Gospel Advocate Co., 1988).

I have not abandoned contexts; who, to whom, and circumstances are all important. But the principle behind the command and the motive of the heart has helped me to answer a lot of the why questions. When I was a teen sitting rebelliously in a Bible class I would rather have not attended, I wore my teacher out with "Why?" Kenneth, bless his heart, hated to see me come to class as much as I hated to be there. Yet he was patient with me and put up with the why questions. Getting away from me may have been one of the reasons that he left to go to a school of biblical studies. The why questions, however, continued to haunt me. There are, of course, some questions that are a matter of faith. Some ideas, as I have come to believe, transcend questioning. Faith responds to those questions with confidence in the Lord's sovereignty to simply believe. But the Lord did not give us a mind and then expect us to write off everything as a matter of faith. He chooses for us to study and pray, to hunger and thirst for righteousness, and to seek and we shall find. It is to those questions of hungering, thirsting, and seeking that study and prayer are applied.

In this study, I hope to use the principle behind the command in a way that can be as useful to you as it has been to me. Jesus preached the sermon to change the actions of those who followed Him. Yet He not only wanted to change the actions of the Jewish believer but also to change their attitude as well. If actions were all He was interested in, then He could have created a computerized, preprogrammed android of the movie variety on the sixth day instead of a free-willed, choice-oriented, emotion-filled human being. So instead of the android, He made Adam. The reason He made Adam is a God thing. He made humans so that when we choose to be faithful rather than being forced to be faithful, God will be glorified. If the changing of actions on the part of humans were all that the Lord Creator is interested in, then robots would have sufficed. Rather, the Lord desires more than just a rearranging of lifestyles to conform to His will. He wants His people to change their hearts and attitudes. He wants us to desire, want, long, and do His will. When this occurs, then the actions will most definitely follow. So this study of the sermon will look at the attitude behind the action because when the attitude is changed, the action will follow.

These precepts of the Lord are commands. That will not change. The sermon is not optional. It is not an elective in His university of maturity. The commands may be difficult for you. They may stretch you like a rubber band, like it did me. But if we can try to understand the principle behind the command and change our view of the reasons these commands are important, then we may be able to see more clearly the holiness of the heart of God and draw our love and affection toward Him in a more realistic way. If this can occur, a freshness, a delight, an attitude that passes understanding will motivate our conformity to Him and His will that no one or nothing can undermine. We then can experience Jesus's statements "My yoke is easy, and my burden is light" and "You shall find rest for your souls." (Matthew 11:28-30). This adds new meaning to "taste and see that the Lord is good." (Psalm 38:8).

This book is not an exhaustive, exegetical analysis of the Greek meanings along with word studies and exciting illustrations that will wow your soul. This prose is simply a commentary of my prayer and study intended not as an authoritarian mandate of the way it is, but rather as my subjective study for your perusal. I hope you are intrigued to the point that you continue to contemplate and meditate on its concepts.

THE BEATITUDES

Blessed are the poor in spirit, for theirs is the kingdom of heaven.

Blessed are those who mourn, for they will be comforted.

Blessed are the meek, for they will inherit the earth.

Blessed are those who hunger and thirst for righteousness, for they will be filled.

Blessed are the merciful, for they will be shown mercy.

Blessed are the pure in heart, for they will see God.

Blessed are the peacemakers, for they will be called sons of God.

Blessed are those who are persecuted because of righteousness, for theirs is the kingdom of heaven.

Blessed are you when people insult you, persecute you and falsely say all kinds of evil against you because of me.

Rejoice and be glad, because great is your reward in heaven, for in the same way they persecuted the prophets that were before you. (Matthew 5:3–12)

Verses 3–12 of the sermon are an indication of the radical nature of what Jesus is trying to teach. These verses are not some unrelated religious suggestions that sound poetic and preachy, but rather, they are a methodology to the maturity the Lord intends. They are steps to growth. In verses 3–12, you will find a progression of growth that, I believe, Jesus used to build His disciples' faith and maturity.

It begins with the poor in spirit and ends with the persecuted. It carries with it steps to maturity that are sprinkled throughout the remainder of the sermon. Each aspect of the sermon requires different elements of the beatitudes or even all of them. As you begin this journey through the sermon again, try to see the maturity of the beatitudes that are related to each section.

This can be a life-changing experience. It can continue to be a life-changing experience. I pray that mine continues to change. I pray that you do too.

ONE

The Poor in Spirit–Attitude toward God

Blessed are the poor in spirit, for theirs is the kingdom of heaven.
– MATTHEW 5:3

The heart of all that Jesus taught is encapsulated in the attitude of being poor in spirit. "Poor in spirit" is the foundation of everything that involves the unique relationship of man to God. "Poor in spirit" is the Lord's purpose behind everything He teaches. Without it, no honest, pure submission can occur in any aspect of following the will of God. So it is my understanding that "poor in spirit" becomes the focal point of any attempt to change or be changed.

Without going into a deep analytical explanation from the original language as to the exact meaning of "poor in spirit," let me pass to those more qualified. But with those scholars in mind, it is the consensus that "poor in spirit" simply means "humble."[12] Humility is the foundation of salvation (James 4:6).[3] It is through humility that grace is enacted by the God of all grace.

Humility is an attitude of the heart. It reflects not only my opinion of my own state, but more importantly, it reflects my attitude toward God. It is the initial challenge that Jesus offers to His people as the basis of everything else He has to say. If I think too highly of myself, then I cannot submit to what He has to offer. If I think too little of myself, I cannot assume the role that He intends for my life. Humility suggests that I do not think of myself as humility places God where He should be, at the center of the universe. Everything revolves around Him. The Hebrew writer puts it this way: "It was fitting that God, for whom and through whom everything exists" (Hebrews 2:10). Everything in the universe exists for His glory. Humility of the heart assumes that my position is not being the center of the universe. Everything does not revolve around me. Everything revolves around God.

---

[2] Class notes, "Sermon on the Mount," instructor Ted Kell (Sunset School of Preaching, Lubbock, Texas, September 9, 1978). Sunset School of Preaching is now the Sunset International Bible Institute.

[3] James 4:6 "God opposes the proud but gives grace to the humble," quoted from Proverbs 3:34.

"Poor in spirit" endeavors to relate that God is the central focus and I am a created being here to do His bidding for His glory.

Some may tend to see this as a bit demeaning to the excellence of humanity if there is such a thing as the excellence of humanity. I suggest it is not demeaning or degrading at all. If my vision of myself blocks my vision of God, then I cannot implement His will in my life because my concern for myself outweighs my concern for God's will. This is an essential element in growth. If my concern or what is best for me collides with what God knows is best for me, then there is a choice to be made. Humility allows for a choice to be made with God being the central focus. Humility allows that choice to be made according to what He wants and not according to what I want or what is comfortable to me.

Being poor in spirit is essential in the formation of the maturity of the disciple. Its foundation is the necessity for the building of the relationship with the Father who produces growth. Without humility, the things that are necessary to move toward Him cannot flourish. If my willingness for self-determination is the end and what I want is the means to that end, then God's will for me is not seen in the high regard that He intends. When the humility of my heart becomes a suggestion, rather than a necessity, then everything else is misplaced and becomes blurry. If humility is not consistent with my attitude, then my submission to Him is not the priority; it is the option. When humility is of little value, then the directives of Jesus that are intended for my maturity are ignored as being unnecessary, too difficult, or wrong for me.

But on the other hand, if humility is a vital concern in my life, then God's will becomes the priority. Humility lines up the lenses and brings everything else into a sharp, focused, crystal-clear image. Humility brings a submission that is never forced, demanded, or deemed optional. The humble heart embraces

Jesus's words without weighing the necessity, the difficulty, or what is right for me.

Humility is the basis not only for the Sermon on the Mount, but also for the whole of Jesus's teachings. Humility reflects the attitude concerning God. This is the point of humility. Being poor in spirit lifts God to a higher plane in my eyes. It reflects an attitude of my heart, which honors Him above everything else. Humility does not put me in the gutter. It lifts the Lord. It exalts Him not only as God but also as Creator and the Father who knows best.

The attitude of humility ensures dependence upon Him. It eliminates dependence upon me. This attitude is freeing. It takes life out of the realm of chance and places it into the realm of God. Worry, anxiety, and concerns all take on a new, less-important meaning as we will see as our study progresses. Humility enhances faith. It assumes that we can entrust our lives into His hands because of Him. This causes belief to increase as He continues to be faithful in His promises. One builds on the other. Humility causes me to depend on Him, and as He constantly proves Himself to be dependable, my faith continues to grow, which reinforces who He is and who I am in relation to Him.

Humility is an attitude of the heart. It reflects not only my opinion of my own state but more importantly, it reflects my attitude toward God. Pride is the selfish nature that I learned as a child. Pride is the thing that makes my world revolve around me. Pride is opposed to everything that God stands for in my life. Pride produces rebellion. Pride colors everything I encounter. Pride shades my character. Pride prohibits trust. Pride defies anything that makes me uncomfortable. Pride will keep me from submission. That is why humility is so important. Humility cannot coexist with pride. It is an either/or situation; it is one or the other, and so are their effects. Humility absorbs God's things while pride repels them. Humility invites submission to God's will while pride breeds rebellion. Humility is to submission as pride is to rebellion. Humility brings one and pride brings the other. They are as opposed to each other as light is to darkness. That is the one reason humility of the heart is so important in my relationship with God. It allows me to submit to Him as the ultimate authority.

As I consider the beatitudes found in Matthew 5, I believe humility, being poor in spirit, to be the foundation of the rest. The beatitudes are not a menagerie of nice one-liners but the Lord's recipe for discipleship. Each one builds on what comes before. All are based on the foundation of humility. If I find myself having problems with any of His steps, then I need to go back to the foundation, poor in spirit. This serves as the watermark from which everything else is measured.

Growth in Christ is not something that is obtained by osmosis. I cannot simply wake up one morning and be a soul winner or be one who can take joy in difficulties as the means of maturity. Christian growth has a specific plan laid by the ultimate in maturity. For me to become what He wants and follow in His steps, I must first follow His directives. To better understand this concept of disciple-building from the sermon, first try to look at the beatitudes in a different way. Instead of reading them from top to bottom, try to think of them from bottom to top. "Poor in spirit" is the first in the stack. Mourning is the second. Meekness is the third. Hungering and thirsting are the fourth. The list goes on. When I have a problem dealing with any of the steps, I go back to the beginning and see where my humility stands.

In Christian growth, one great disadvantage that has been an unfortunate constant in my life is self-righteousness. Self-righteousness stems from pride. Whenever I try to determine my level of growth, there is always a tendency to stick my thumbs under my suspenders and take pride In such an accomplishment. At that point, humility is diminished and my attitude toward

God changes from dependence on Him to esteem for me. My growth no longer is a result of what He has done in my life, but rather what I have accomplished. That is the danger of growth assessment. Realizing growth can sometimes lead to a sense of accomplishment. When that occurs, it is usually humility that suffers. When humility suffers, the entire process breaks down.

Everything is built on my attitude toward God. If that attitude toward Him becomes faulty, then the chain is broken and my vision of Him is blurred. Humility is the attitude that keeps my focus on Him intact and my growth moving. This is the reason I must always go back to the bottom line, and that is to maintain the correct attitude toward God. Humility is an instrument for maintenance or correction.

The attitude of the poor in spirit points out not only my need for Him but continues to show me my dependence on Him. It inevitably points out His greatness and worth, and my weakness without Him. From this humility come the building blocks that lead to maturity. The next step, although basic, is necessary. Jesus describes it this way: "Blessed are those who mourn." This attitude of mourning follows the realization of the holiness of God and leads to my intense need for Him.

TWO

Those Who Mourn—Attitude toward Sin

Blessed are those who mourn, for they will be comforted.
—MATTHEW 5:4

The concept of mourning is not very appealing. We usually associate mourning with death. The passing of a loved one or friend causes me to be extremely sorrowful, and the result is a heartfelt, mournful emotion. I do not believe that Jesus is trying to develop in me an attitude of self-pity that brings a blessing or invokes a reward for a mournful countenance when we are hurting on the inside. I believe that mourning is for a state that we find ourselves in because of our human condition. That human condition is sin. Since our attitude toward God is humility toward Him, we now turn to the reason we are so awed by Him. Our condition is sinfulness, His existence is holy, and He *still* desires to have a relationship with us. Our response to that circumstance is overwhelming because of Him but sorrowful because of us. That sorrow is for our sin.

If we cannot understand that our plight is one of not being able to live up to all that He intended for us to be, we cannot progress in our maturity. If we *do* believe that we are all that we can be, then there is no need or reason for growth. It is the sin problem that brought the Son into the world. If we could have corrected the problem on our own, then He would not have had to come as a man and defeat the Defeater for us. Since He did come, we do understand that salvation is not in our individual or collective abilities. Our relationship with God is not determined by us; it is determined by what Jesus did.

The reason that I am awkward in relating to the Holy God of the universe is one thing and one thing alone: sin. If I realize this, then it sets the tone for the remainder of my Christian experience. My response in humility to who I am, and to who He is, is to be sorry for the sin that is in my life. It is not simply to be sorry but rather to mourn. If I am not deeply remorseful to the point of mourning for my sin, then correcting the situation is out of the question.

We need to understand who the folks are Jesus is speaking to in this passage. He is preaching to Jews. They were, at that time, the covenant children of God. They had, by birth, a relationship with God by way of their blood tie to Abraham. They were already His people. The time had come. Just being a blood relative of Abraham was no longer enough. There was now a need for something more. There was a need to change. There was a need for a change of heart to maintain the covenant relationship with God. So the maintenance of that relationship necessitated a change in action. Jesus chose to change that action by first changing the attitude. Their pride in Abraham, Isaac, and Jacob as their lineage was, in their view, the only thing that they needed. Jesus was helping them understand that there was a problem. Even amid a divine decree of blood relation by Abraham, there was a problem. That problem was sin. We are not talking about salvation here on the Mount; rather, we are talking about relationship. Yes, the sin problem had to be dealt with, and indeed it would be. Calvary would be the ultimate battleground, and the open tomb would be the peace treaty. Yet after the blood of Jesus initially establishes the relationship in my life, I, like the Jews, still must deal with sin in my life. To ignore that a continual change, then, is necessary to maintain a relationship with the Lord of the universe is to ignore and even deny that there is a problem in my life with sin.

If I do not see myself as a covenant child of God who does not add up to what He wants, then I miss the whole point of maturity. This is the point: If I believe there is nothing to change, if I believe there is no sin to expel, if I believe I am what God wants me to be, then there is no need to mature. I am already there. But if I, in humility, acknowledge there is a problem, if I acknowledge there is room for improvement, if I confess that I am short of what He wants, then maturity can flourish. Sin, in part or in whole, is the one thing that will inhibit my maturity or growth in Christ. It was the same for the Jews. Sin was the problem that kept them from maturity. So for me to be what God wants me to be, I must acknowledge the problem and mourn the fact that even though I am a covenant child of God, I still do not measure up.

Mourning for sin reminds me that there is always room for improvement. If I simply say that there is sin in my life but I do not in actuality believe it, then I not only minimize the sin problem but also do not see a need for growth and change. If I honestly believe that my sin is a source of concern and I am extremely sorry to the point of mourning, then my attitude changes not only toward God but also toward myself. The attitude toward God changes because of His supreme holiness and purity in relation to my sinful nature. The attitude about me changes because I see a desperate need to repent of the sin in my life. Again, one must be humble not only to admit the sin problem but also to mourn because of it. If there is no mourning for sin, then I need to go back to the first level. Blessed are the poor in spirit. The only way to recognize and mourn for sin is to be humble enough to acknowledge that it exists.

Mourning for the sin that is in my life serves as a constant reminder of several things. First, it reminds me who God is. He is holy and pure. He is utterly and undeniably above me and all that I am. Second, it reminds me who I am. The sinful state of my humanity cannot be compared with His awesome nature. His ways are higher than my ways. His thoughts are higher than my thoughts.[4] Third, it reminds me of my intense need for Jesus and the forgiveness that He affords me. Where would I be without Jesus? Last, it reminds me that I must try to eliminate as much of my sinful nature as I can. By this, I mean I choose to try to change

---

[4] "As the heavens are higher than the earth, so are my ways higher than your ways and my thoughts than your thoughts" (Isaiah 55:9).

my actions. This is simply repentance! It does not come by just *doing different things* or *doing things differently.* It comes with a change in attitude first. It is a change of the heart in view of the holiness of God and where I stack up in relation to His holiness. That attitude is repentance for the sin in my life, and mourning of the heart leads to a change in action. For just a moment, let us go back to Isaiah 6:1–5.

> In the year that King Uzziah died, I saw the Lord seated on a throne, high and exalted, and the train of His robe filled the temple. Above Him were seraphim, each with six wings: With two wings they covered their faces, with two they covered their feet, and with two they were flying. And they were calling to one another: "Holy, holy, holy is the Lord Almighty the whole earth is full of His glory." At the sound of their voices the doorposts and the thresholds shook, and the temple was filled with smoke. "Woe to me! I cried. I am ruined! For I am a man of unclean lips, and I live among a people of unclean lips, and my eyes have seen the King, the Lord Almighty."

This is a perfect example of what the holiness of God will do to a person who gets a glimpse of His glory. Isaiah saw the awesomeness of God in His own temple. He saw and heard the angels showing and calling out His holiness. Isaiah's response was that of humility and sorrow for his sinfulness in relation to God's holiness. That is exactly what mourning is for those who are humbled by God's nature.

Mourning then leads to the next level of growth. When I am able, through humility, to mourn because of the sin in my life, then I am at a place where I see a need for change in my life. When

I come to this realization, I have begun the maturity process by changing both my attitude toward God (poor in spirit) and my attitude toward sin (mourning). These two attitude changes make for something new in my life. Jesus put it this way. Blessed are the meek.

THREE

The Meek–Attitude toward Discipline

Blessed are the meek, for they
will inherit the earth.
–MATTHEW 5:5

D on retired from a federal agency in the early to mid-1970s.[5] Between classes, he used to tell stories of his years growing up in Colorado. He told of one summer that caught my interest. This former federal employee turned preacher once lived the life of a cowboy. He rode the range in search of wild mustangs to round up and bring to a ranch. Don spoke of sleeping under a Colorado sky, campfires, and living a real-life western. He told stories of escapades that would evoke the imagination of a twenty-three-year-old young man to think on those days with envy and amazement. Yet the thing that I remember most of Don's stories was breaking a wild horse. This was not a horse that had been born and bred on a West Virginia farm and reared with oats, hay, and pasture grass. It was a creature of the wild that was tamed. He used breathtaking descriptions that made me sit with eyes wide and round. His Wild West experience made a particular impact on me. As I began studying the concept of meekness, Don's story helped me to understand, and I hope it will help you too.

Meekness is a concept that is very often misunderstood. Many folks in our society equate meekness with weakness. Timidity is another word that may also come to mind. Some may characterize a meek person as one who is too timid or afraid to speak or act when injustice is occurring in their lives. Meekness has been depicted as a person with a mixture of somberness and sadness on his face. But meekness is anything but weak and timid. Meekness is just the opposite. It is power that is controlled.[6]

In the story of the wild mustangs, the idea of meekness was brought to my mind as Don described the muscles rippling in the

5 Don was a classmate at the Sunset School of Preaching from 1977 to 1979. He retired from the federal government prior to attending Sunset School of Preaching. He became a preacher after his graduation.

6 Class Notes, "Sermon on the Mount," Instructor Ted Kell, (Sunset School of Preaching, Lubbock, Texas, September 12, 1978).

shoulders of those horses. The power they displayed seemed to be concentrated because of their wild nature. Yet they were tamed by the trainer. The key word here is *tamed*. When a horse is tamed, is he any less powerful? Of course, the answer is no. He is no less powerful. He is now under control. That power has been harnessed to be useful. That power is channeled or directed in a different way. Likewise, meekness is the attitude toward discipline.

In following the steps that Jesus taught to become a disciple, this is the next level that one of His followers would pursue. When the poor in spirit become sorry for their sin, they would logically try to alter their lifestyle that conflicts with the will of the Father. Jesus wants us to learn to control or discipline ourselves. Meekness is to change the things about myself that interfere with what He wants for me in my life. To say it simply, He wants me to be tame so that sin is not the rule of my life. Does this mean that I am any less powerful in and of myself? No! Does this take the passion of life away? Of course, it does not! Does it mean that I show no feeling or emotion? Again no, meekness simply means that I want the divine trainer to tame me. When I realize that sin is in direct opposition to the awesome God of the universe and I become mournful of the fact that my human condition wants to do what I want, I must do something to control the very thing that is in opposition to God. That is what meekness is. It is controlling my sinful nature to do the will of the Father, rather than doing what I want. This third step in the Lord's recipe for discipleship is sometimes rearranged in sequence. It is only when I am poor in spirit and mourning for my sin that the concept of control can be willingly enacted. Willing—that is the key word.

Preachers can preach until they are blue in the face about all the *cans* and *cannots* of what God wants. I can be dangled over the bottomless pit to force conformity to God's will. But conformity is not what God is after. If conformity was all that He desired, then

He could have made non-willed entities to conform to His will. He is after faithfulness, and that faithfulness is intended to be chosen *willingly.*

This is a big deal! It has been my experience, not only in my preaching but also in the ministries of others, that control and discipline are mandated at the beginning. From our instruction, it is a necessity of God from the start. The reason this is preached so often and so demandingly may be because it is so easy to preach. It is much easier for me to be assertive and forthright about telling folks what to do and what not to do than to lead them to a level of maturity where they, of their own free choice, choose to follow God's will. It is like the difference between knowing facts about God and knowing God. This concept of meekness from mourning from humility is a big deal.

Here is a disclaimer. I do not deny that God wants obedience. If you think that I am saying that He does not want obedience, then you have misunderstood. He wants us to follow His directives. That is His will. But He does not want us to simply conform or obey for the sake of *making others think* that we are being obedient. I heard a preacher use this illustration one time. I do not know where he got it. Anyway, it will serve here nicely. This young mother had a defiant young little son on her hands. He had done something to incur the wrath of his momma. She told him to sit down in a chair. He said no. Well, if I told my, mother no when she told me to sit down, I would not have to worry about sitting down. Anyway, this mother was a patient woman. She kept her composure and told him again. He again refused. She calmly walked over to him and sat him down in the chair. He defiantly looked at her and said, "I may be sitting down on the outside, but I'm standing up on the inside."

This is conformity. Preaching dos and do-nots lends itself to Christians who sit down on the outside but stand up on the inside.

No one can tell the difference. No one can determine if they want to or do not want to. They sing the right songs. They pray for the right words. They do all the churchy things and wear all the churchy clothes. They nod in the churchy way, but in their hearts, they are standing up. No one knows the difference. Everyone thinks that they have it all together. No one knows their lives are falling apart. No one knows they are miserable. No one knows. Unfortunately for us, God knows, and He is the one that matters. That is what Jesus was trying to change in the first century and in the twenty-first century.

God wants us to want to do His will. Jim McGuiggan[7] first introduced me to the concept of *wanting* to do God's will as opposed to *having* to do God's will. Jim's plow, of course, goes much deeper than mine does, but I did get this nugget from the field. I am missing the joy of serving God if I am only in it because I *must* be. This is where the sermon is so different, so radical. Jesus helps us lay the groundwork for desire. It starts with humility (who God is) then goes to mourning (who I am) and then to meekness (I need to change).

Meekness is the place where need meets longing. I know from my mourning and poor spirit that I need to change. Meekness is the place where I begin to want to change. I begin to want to control myself because I lack control in my life. I do not need to be forced. I do not want to be forced. I want, I desire, I long to be controlled. What a weight is taken off my shoulders when meekness is fostered. What a delight submitting becomes. Meekness changes everything. The chains of religion's prohibitions are exchanged for God's pleasures. Meekness is the point where the ripples of the spiritual muscles go from the concentrated wildness of the open range to the taming of the divine trainer: bridled, saddled, and

---

[7]   Jim McGuiggan, instructor (Sunset School of Preaching, Lubbock, Texas, 1977–1979), author of over twenty commentaries and books.

useful for His purposes. I can still run just as fast. I can still snort and snicker with the best of them. I can kick up my heels just as high as I could before. The difference is that now someone else is in the saddle. The King has hold of the reins. I go where He wants. I go as fast as He wants or as slow as He wants. The key is I go under His control and am willing to do it. This is meekness.

The best example of meekness that has ever been displayed came one time outside of Jerusalem in a garden called Gethsemane. The prayers were finished. The ground was red with sweat. The torches lit up the path. Peter pulled his sword. The Creator could have called it all off. He could have chosen to snap His fingers and twelve legions of angels would have been in fighting formation marking time, waiting for the command. Yet He chose not to. He chose to be meek. He had the power of the universe at His breath. He was under control because the prayer He prayed was the prayer of the humble. Meekness chooses the Father's will. Meekness chooses "Not my will but thine." Was Jesus any less powerful? Was He timid? Was He weak? You know He was not. He was meek! What strength! What control! Lord, help me to be like you.

FOUR

Hunger and Thirst–
Attitude toward Desire

Blessed are those who hunger and thirst
for righteousness, for they will be filled.
–MATTHEW 5:6

There is no need more basic to man than hunger and thirst. Go on a diet. Work outside on a one-hundred-degree day. See if you do not agree. But most of the time, in my life, hunger and thirst are not things that normally attract the biggest part of my attention. I have never been too hungry or too thirsty. In the context of the sermon, hungering and thirsting are not some physical desires to appease a craving of my body. "Hungering and thirsting" relates to a craving of the soul. This craving is for righteousness.

The desire for righteousness is the natural response of a humble soul that has admitted and mourned because of the inhabitation of sin. The soul then sees a need for control but does not know how to control what is not understood. This is where righteousness comes in. Righteousness is what the humble, mourning, need-for-control soul longs for. This hunger and thirst for righteousness goes to the very heart of serving God. Hungering and thirsting are the motives of the disciples of the Lord. It is the desire from within to do what is right.

Doing what is right is not a forcible issue. Although doing right is what we really want to do as children of the King. It is not God's will to put His foot on our necks until we cry uncle and submit to Him. This desire has been cultivated by humility. It has been grown through mourning. It has been developed by meekness. This is where the desire to do God's will unfolds in the believer's life.

Everything that follows in a disciple's journey is predicated on why he does what he does. The reason for following God's will is all-important. It is the difference between an honest, Cross-centered believer and one who follows conveniently. The desire for rightness transcends mere ritualistic religion. The desire for righteousness is the thing that attempts to do what is right, even when no one else is watching. When no one on this earth would know the difference in whether we submit to God's will or get away with something, the desire for righteousness always inwardly tugs us back to God's will. The remainder of the maturing process depends upon whether this desire is nurtured.

The motive for doing God's will is a key to believers' growth. It goes to the heart of what I want. If a desire for righteousness is never fostered, then my time is spent on outward appearance. I am then more attuned to what others think, rather than to what God wants. This was a paramount issue to the ones to whom Jesus was speaking on the mount. They saw the rulers of the Jews, the scribes, the Pharisees, and the Sadducees jockeying for position as to which sect had the most influence over the people. Their method of influence was not righteousness. It was the perception of others' righteousness. Jesus, on several occasions, blasted them for being pretty and refined on the outside but black and ugly on the inside. They were like graves at a cemetery. The cemetery looked very beautiful, but that which was buried beneath the sod was rotten to the core.[8]

The call for hungering and thirsting for righteousness counteracts the concept that righteousness is only what others perceive in me. This desire of hungering and thirsting germinates from the recognition that I cannot do it on my own. I need some guidance in this discipline if I am going to change the rule of sin in my life. This is the desire for training from some place other than my own thought processes. When I finally admit and am sorry for the sin in my life, I confess that I need something other than myself. When I want the control to change from me to God, I realize that He is the one who must give me the guidance I need

---

[8]   "Woe to you, teachers of the law and Pharisees, you hypocrites! You are like whitewashed tombs, which look beautiful on the outside but on the inside are full of dead men's bones and everything unclean." (Matthew 23:27)

for the change to take place. This is the hungering-and-thirsting mode.

The standard for righteousness is not something that is legislated by men. Neither does it come from a poll of eligible voters. The standard for righteousness is found only through God, who created us. He is the only one who knows the standard because He is the standard of righteousness. Righteousness is based on His nature. Since His nature is righteous, He made the standard of righteousness. Since He created righteousness and us, He knows how we should function. It comes only from His place, from His nature, from His mouth. It is His word. God communicated His will *for* us *to* us. His word is the standard for righteousness. Without His word, we would be left to ourselves to develop the standard of righteousness. If that were the case, there would be a plethora of righteousness standards. Some try to insist each instance of life has its own standard of righteousness and each instance would be dependent upon a multitude of circumstances. But this is not the case.

We have in God's word a model of righteousness communicated to us. This is the source of the training that we need to change our mournful ways. It is through His word that we can ascertain what righteousness is. The desire for this to be added to our lives does not come by mere proximity to His word. It comes from a desire to study His word to find out how we should live and do the right things with our lives. It comes from a desire to pray to the Father, asking Him to lead us into righteousness through His Holy Spirit (Romans 8:9–14). It comes by imitating folks who have been trained by God in righteousness (Hebrews 13:7–8).

This desire for righteousness does not replace humility, mourning, and meekness. This desire for righteousness is the result of them. Yet there is a trap, and if we trip the wire, everything will explode. Do not confuse the desire for righteousness with self-righteousness. Therefore, we consider that righteousness is of God and not of ourselves. We are not trying to have a stained-glass righteousness like the Pharisees. We are trying to learn to do the right thing in life. We are trying to let God's standard be the standard that is implemented to alter our lives, for which we mourn. It is letting God's standard be the standard that we use to control the power to choose what He has given us.

When this desire blooms, then there will be no need for anyone to challenge me to study my Bible. There will be no need for anyone to challenge me to grow in my prayer life. There will be no need for the preacher to constantly remind me to do the right thing. I will already have the desire to study, pray, and try to do the right things before God. I will have the desire for rightness. I will have a hungering and thirsting that cannot be coerced. That is not a guilt-trip experience. It is a life-giving experience. It is the motive that goes deeper than guilt and fear. It is a motive that comes from within to please the one to whom I owe my existence in Christ.

We have looked at four steps in the maturing process. All four deal with me. The four deal with the idea of "changing me." There is no mention of others. The next step turns toward them. It is the logical next step because I must live in this world with others. I am not alone and not intending to be alone. So what do humility, repentance, control, and desire for righteousness have to do with others? It leads us to be merciful.

FIVE

The Merciful–Attitude toward Others

Blessed are the merciful, for
they will be shown mercy.
–MATTHEW 5:7

There is something about mercy that is rooted far deeper than man's imagination. Mercy is not something that is an everyday, normal, run-of-the-mill concept. It far outweighs the depths of my consideration or contemplation. It does not have its origins in humanity, nor has it been finely tuned by man's intellect. Mercy is something that began in the heart of God. He then communicated it to us and showed us. He is the only way we could have known anything about mercy. To assume anything otherwise is to be presumptive and arrogant. Mercy is as much opposed to man's nature as sin is the opposite of holiness. It only comes from an understanding of God, of myself, of my need for change, and of my desire for His righteousness revealed to me. It only comes through maturity. Therefore, mercy is the next step of discipleship.

When Jesus taught on the mount, He spoke to folks who were steeped in an *eye-for-an-eye* religion. That was not bad, you see. It was the eye-for-an-eye religion that kept Israel together as a people until Christ should come (Galatians 3:19). It was the teacher that would lead them to understand they could not save themselves. So this eye-for-an-eye religion had its place in God's grand scheme. Jesus, now, is changing everything. They were not accustomed to mercy, forgiveness, and forbearance because that was not the tradition of the teachers of the law. Jesus was introducing concepts that were foreign to their thinking and practice. Among those concepts was the idea of being merciful.

Mercy carries with it the idea of forgiveness and forbearance. It does not excuse, overlook, or sweep anything under the carpet. It is simply mercy. Mercy acknowledges that there is a problem. The problem is sin. Mercy just does not require the guilty to receive the deserved punishment. That really sounds good. My thought is "I want that!" The fact is, God has already given me that! Now, mercy does not contradict God's Holiness; it exposes it.

God, being holy, must punish sin. That is part of His holy nature. He, however, chose to punish sin in Jesus (Romans 3:25–26). The justness or justice of God's holiness is satisfied in Jesus's being punished for my sin on the cross.

In the context of the sermon, the merciful are those who have already received mercy being called upon to extend mercy to others who need mercy. The attitude behind the directive addressed in this context is the attitude toward others. It is only when we have seen ourselves in relation to God and found out by His will what rightness is that we can turn our attention to others. This is the maturity process Jesus is calling for.

It is extremely difficult to be merciful when a disciple has not seen the mercy that has been given to him. This is the reason the first four steps are so critical in the growth process. If we do not, in humility (poor in spirit), see ourselves as needing much mercy (mourn) and try to tame our lives (meek) desiring the standard of His revealed righteousness (hunger and thirst after righteousness), then we will not see the need of being merciful to others *who are in the same condition that we are in.* Outside of God, the only ones who can or will extend mercy are those who realize that they have received mercy.

Many people who do not see themselves as needing mercy will not be willing to give mercy. Some demand of others what they think they have already attained. If others do not meet that expectation, then a consequence must follow. This merciless concept stems from the opposite of the first four of the beatitudes. The opposite of being poor in spirit/humility is pride. The opposite of mourning/remorse is denial. The opposite of meekness/discipline is perpetuation. The opposite of hunger and thirsting after righteousness/desire is self-righteousness.

Pride leads to denial.
Denial fosters perpetuation.
Perpetuation breeds self-righteousness.
Self-righteousness prohibits mercy.

This is a fair description of the Pharisees. Unfortunately, it is at times, a fair description of me too. This is what the folks on the mount thought religion to be. This was what they had seen. This was what they were taught. This is what they practiced. The Gospels are full of folks who are unmerciful, and they condemned Jesus for acting differently from them.

For followers of Jesus to become what He wants, mercy must be an integral part of the equation. This is where the focus turns from our needs to the needs of others. Mercy is the point where we see others *as we are* instead of seeing them in relation to where *we think we are*. Comparisons always seem to get the best of growth. It inhibits and even prohibits maturity. Comparisons ignore the first four steps of maturity. When I compare others with my self-righteousness, they always come up lacking. When I see them lacking, I demand more of them. When I demand more of them, I am less likely to be merciful.

Comparisons are not bad if we can compare the right things. The comparison that presupposes mercy is the comparison of my life to God's. This is the first step again, poor in spirit. God's righteousness cannot coexist with self-righteousness. When the comparison of holy God is made to sinful me, then self-righteousness ceases. It is only when my nature is compared with God's nature that I can then look at others with the proper perspective. If I do not make this comparison, then mercy is not to be found in my understanding. This comparison sets up the ultimate reality check. This is the only way that I can really see others. They are exactly like me, in desperate need of mercy.

When I understand that others need mercy as much as I do, then mercy can be freely given to anyone who bears the need.

Being merciful to others is the next level of maturity. It is at this level that we begin to transcend our nature and become partakers of the divine nature because mercy is rooted in God's heart, in His nature. Mercy is the level of maturity where God's kind of love begins to be shown in the lives of the believers. Mercy is where pronouns and vowels are switched. *I* changes to *you*. Mercy is the transition from *me* to *them*. Mercy is the place where God allows me to take from Him and give to them. Mercy is the place where I begin to understand that Jesus has already taken the punishment for my sins and for the sins of others. Since other believers' sins have been punished in the death of Jesus on the cross (the same as mine) and received mercy from the Father because of that (the same as me) then I can extend mercy to them and be just in doing it, just like the Father.

This plateau is only met when the first four steps come to pass in our lives. Unfortunately, many have tried to require young believers to live on this level before their time. Many found it too difficult. They wept at their insufficiency. They wept, but they still left for an easier path.

This is not easy. Jesus never said it would be. We, as believers, should not make it out to be easy. Maturity is difficult; it really is. Take heart though, believer in Jesus, because as the growth process continues, it gets tougher.

SIX

The Pure in Heart–Attitude toward Heart

Blessed are the pure in heart,
for they will see God.
–MATTHEW 5:8

P urity is a beautiful word. It brings to mind images of white. It brings to mind thoughts of sincerity and goodness. It makes me feel good just thinking of purity. *Pure* is an adjective that describes something. Pure is associated with many things. It describes things like water, wool, brides, newborn babies, the country air that I breathe, and many other things that we want to be clean, clear, and perfect. When we look at this next level of discipleship, we can be too taken by the concept of purity and miss the whole issue.

The issue here is not purity. It is the heart. It is the emotional center of our soul. The heart is the one thing in our lives that in reality rules what we do. Tim LaHaye has a nice discussion in his book *The Battle for the Mind* that is worth reading. He says that everything we do is filtered through the emotional center. The memory we have stored, the decisions of the will, the actions that we take are first and finally filtered through the heart [9] That is why the heart is so important in the maturity process.

The heart is involved from the very beginning of our spiritual journey. Pride and humility are attitudes of the heart. Repentance and continuance are filtered through the heart. Control and free rein also flow through this part of our soul. Mercy and demand both are affected by it. Yet why does the heart play such a significant role here?

The answer comes from the Lord's descriptive term that accompanies it. He wants the heart to be pure. He wants us to be honest in the way we look at ourselves and at others. He wants our service to be sincere to Him. He wants our actions, which are decided by the heart, to be willing. This heart thing is indeed a big deal. God is not interested in His followers being on a strictly intellectual plane. Although following God and learning

---

[9]   Tim LaHaye, *The Battle for the Mind* (Old Tappan, New Jersey: Flemming H. Revell Co., 1980), p. 16–22.

of Him is intellectual, a man does not have to park his brain to be a Christian. Most of the greatest intellectual minds that have ever lived were believers. The intellect that He placed inside us must be involved to digest His will for us. But intellect alone does not produce action.

The interests of God are not found in our intellectual exegesis but rather in our heart's response to Him. The heart is what controls. If the heart is foreign to faith, then worship, serving, and any other aspect of our relationship to God is mere formality. This is the context of the sermon. The Pharisees knew the law. They pondered it, manipulated it, and kept it. Their intellectual digestion was impeccable. But their intellectual digestion made God sick to His stomach. Their problem was not intellectual. They honored God with their lips. It was right to honor God with their lips. It was very right. Yet they were condemned because their heart was far from Him.[10] The problem was not their intellectual relationship. Their problem was the impurity of their heart.

The purity of the heart keeps the disciple who has been merciful from continuing to be merciful. The pure heart honors God at all costs. The pure heart leaves others' baggage of days gone by, behind. Pure hearts are honest in the present tense whenever the tense is present. Purity of the heart is a moment-by-moment thing. It is not something that happens once and then is good for the duration. It is a continuous thing, for no matter how much we guard, how much we lie in wait for impurity, waiting for its very inception, the heart can be fooled!

This is the impurity. This is the caution the disciple must always face. The fact is that in our self-assessment, we may be too generous or too lenient with ourselves. Here is where the purity of the heart leads us to be always honest, noble, truthful,

---

[10]   "These people honor me with their lips, but their hearts are far from me." (Matthew 15:8)

and right in the conscious determination of where we are in our maturity. If we are too strict in our own tolerance of ourselves, we lose the divine luster of grace. If we are too lenient in our lives, we become judgmental of others. Purity of the heart is the fine line that balances us.

This is the constant measuring place. Here is where motives meet determination. Here is where willingness meets action. Purity of the heart is a defining place. Without purity of heart, the glimpse of God is gone. This keeps our relationship with God neither in the past nor in the future but just where He wants it, in the present. Purity of heart takes what we started with in changing our attitudes about our lives from pride to humility, from complacency to repentance, from undisciplined to controlled, from having to wanting, to the plane where others take precedence and mercy is offered as we have received it.

The pure heart is the only means to maintain this plateau of growth. The pure heart is the only way to continue in maturity as well. It is when impurity and dishonesty take free rein that the gains are erased, and we begin again with humility. It is amazing to me how each builds on the other and they are so perfectly woven together. It is mind-boggling how such delicate concepts as humility, mourning, meekness, hungering and thirsting, mercy, and purity can be dovetailed to make such a massive, monumental tower of strength. That is exactly what the Lord has done in developing His disciples. Before He goes further, He wants us to make sure that we understand that purity of heart is set in living stone as a benchmark for us to constantly look at our lives in relation to Him and to others. This is also the stepping stone that leads to the next level.

Pure hearts are also what simply keep us on track. A pure heart allows us to regroup. If impure attitudes creep in, we cannot backtrack at all. We cannot admit defeat. We cannot reconcile.

Impurity demands that we forge on amid miscalculation because we must keep up the dreaded pretense of righteousness. Herein lies the point. Impurity cannot admit to anything less than what is right. If it does admit it, then it must have been wrong. There is no way to say, "I am sorry." There is no way to repent. There is no way of escape from being wrong. So to maintain that pretense of righteousness, everything must be manipulated to justify our actions. Everything must be maneuvered to conform to my miscalculation. When I begin this bit of impurity, it is just like the proverbial snowball. There is no stopping it. It translates to others becoming judgmental and unmerciful. It translates to God in the form of self-righteousness and arrogantly determining for others what God wants from their lives. Impurity in the heart is the air brake of the disciple. The growth process stops on a dime, and the engines are in full reverse.

On the other hand, a pure heart is free. Of course, it does not want to be wrong, but it can. It does not want to miscalculate, but it does. It does not want to admit defeat but defeated it will be. It is free. This is the point. The pure heart is continually reassessing. The difference between pure and impure is that when a pure heart realizes it is wrong, it repents. When it miscalculates, it recalculates. When the need for reconciliation is realized, it reconciles. It can backtrack at any time to humility, mourning, control, desire, and mercy. The pure heart is free. There is no pretense in purity—no mask to wear, no costumes to constantly redesign. It is open, honest, and free to follow the pure Christ. A pure heart has only one string attached. That is the thread to the cross. The pure heart can admit wrong, defeat, ineptness, and inadequacy, yet still strive to be right, triumphant, suitable, and full. The pure heart is a benchmark. Without the pure heart, then the heart is not the heart that shall glimpse God. The pure heart is when the disciple can be free to follow at all costs. Will it make mistakes? Will it ever be wrong? Will it be ridiculed? The answer to all the above is yes. The difference is the pure heart will change! That is the beauty of a pure heart. Whenever something impure comes into a pure heart, the pure heart wants it out, whatever it takes. If it takes humility, it is outta there. If it takes repentance, it is gone. If it takes control, then bring on the bits. If it takes willingness, it is removed. The pure heart will always do whatever it takes without any pretense or fanfare. It is always in the present, but it constantly backtracks for change and lunges forward to growth as well. My, my, my, how amazing God is in His infinite wisdom for His followers. Grace in the middle of maturity!

SEVEN

The Peacemaker—Attitude toward Salvation

Blessed are the peacemakers, for they
will be called sons of God.
–MATTHEW 5:9

grew up in the sixties. Now, that is an oxymoron. Well, I grew up in the sixties and seventies. The rebellion, the establishment, the long hair, the music, bell-bottoms, paisley shirts, and all the things we saw on TV were about the extent of this young West Virginian's experience in the sixties and seventies. Those things on TV, well, I had my rebellion and long hair, but I did not have too much time for either. The thing that was a big thing was peace. My generation had visions of the lottery, but it did not have much to do with millions of dollars. It was the draft lottery. We wondered whose birthday was going to be first. Peace seemed like something out of a nineteenth-century-romance novel. We had our ideas of peace. It mostly was the absence of war. It is funny how folks who sought that kind of peace grew to become those folks of the seventies and eighties who started looking for a new kind of peace. Self-help books flooded the market, and the absence of war became the obsession with fulfillment. Peace has always been that way, always just beyond the fingertips.

Peace was the same way with the folks on the mount. Peace is a valuable commodity. The problem is that peace in God's view is something completely different from peace in man's view. One reason that peace is never realized is that peace is a *relationship*, not a premise. God's view of peace is harmony between Him and His creation. Man has not grasped that yet.

This particular attitude of the heart could be understood in a way that Jesus wants His people to be peacemakers among themselves. It may be that Jesus wants us to make peace between friends who are spatting, so they continue to be friends. That is noble; it is highly honorable, it brings good, it helps relationships, and it can glorify God. It may very well be the very thing that Jesus was espousing for the disciple. But I do not think that is what He is climaxing toward in the maturity process. I do not think this is the crescendo of the disciple.

I believe being a peacemaker is a crescendo experience. The magnificence of the experience is not making peace between man and man but making peace between man and God. This is glory. This is the reason the universe was created. It was for God's glory. When peace is made between God and man, then His glory in that life is realized. It is through that relationship that man sees God for who He really is—God! This is the purpose of the disciple, to bring as many as possible to this peace and so God is glorified in their lives as one who loved them and saved them. This is the peacemaker.

In my experience as a Christian and a minister, I must confess that I never saw this placed here in the maturing process. I always wanted new Christians to be evangelistic for the Lord. I prodded. I preached. I used guilt and almost resorted to violence on some occasions trying to get folks to share their faith. I was always trying to get some new study into the hands of folks. They were scared to death. It was a command. We must do it. Well, that was then. This is now. I apologize to the countless numbers of brothers and sisters that I belittled and begged all in the name of evangelism. I am sorry. Although I thought it noble and sharing your faith noble, it was not the Lord's way.

Salvation to the world came from the Lord. He spent three years making disciples, men to whom He said, "Come, follow me and I will make you to become fishers of men." [11] It is a funny thing I missed the "to become" part. It was not when He called Peter that Peter stood up fearlessly in Jerusalem to become a peacemaker. It took three years. It took the maturity process to make him become a peacemaker. So I confess to you now that I have tried to streamline the process. I have mistakenly hurt, abused, chided, and any other term of reproach that I can heap

---

[11] "Come ye after me and I will make you to become fishers of men" (Mark 1:17 American Standard Version).

upon myself to describe what I and thousands of other ministers have done in the name of peacemaking. I have tried to circumvent the Lord's system of peacemaking. I have said all that to say this. His intention is not for the lambs to be thrust before the wolves. His intention is for the mature to do battle. That is why peacemaker is the climax of the beatitudes. It is the attitude toward salvation, not the attitude toward my salvation, although that has everything to do with it. Peacemaking is the attitude toward others' salvation. Remember, when I turned the corner at merciful, the focus left me. The focus turned toward others. The focus of the peacemaker is making peace between God and man.

If we believe in God, if we believe in Jesus and His cross, if we believe that He is the only way, we must acknowledge that anyone who has not come in contact with the blood of Jesus is not at peace with God. If we have come to this point in our maturity, then our faith is to the place that with everything tied together from poor in spirit to pure in heart, we now accept the challenge of bringing the lost to the Lord. It is the role of the teacher. That is what disciples do. Once they have become disciples, they begin to teach to make other disciples.[2] [12]Peacemaker is that role.

Jesus, in His wonderful wisdom, intends for the mature to mature others. It begins by making peace between God and man. It is the intention of Jesus for His believers to tell His story to other people who have not begun this awesome relationship of peace with the Father. He is God. If He wanted to, He could just zap it into every human alive, and there would be no need for each of us to become peacemakers. He really could do that. But He will not do that because it does not bring Him glory. He will not force anyone to love Him.

---

[12] "And the things you have heard me say in the presence of many witnesses entrust to reliable men who will also be qualified to teach others." (2 Timothy 2:2)

What He did do was to love us beyond imagination. He loved us enough to die for us and asked us to tell others about His love. That is His plan. He wants humankind to see Him and His love and *choose* to follow Him because they *want* to. Ahh! This brings Him glory, which is carried out when we tell others the message of peace. We do not choose for them. We just tell them about His peace. It is the disciple of Jesus becoming a teacher, thus, making more disciples of Jesus.

It all goes back to the attitude toward salvation. It is the attitude that salvation to the world concentrates, multiplies, and makes God's glory abound. It is the growth, the maturity of the disciple that makes this possible as a peacemaker. Jesus the Son of God is the ultimate peacemaker on the cross. His disciples who mature into peacemakers come to be called sons of God. It takes humility, remorse, control, desire, mercy, and a pure heart. When this maturity process unfolds, it allows this to happen as naturally as breathing. This is what happens to the disciple as surely as blood coursing through the veins happens when the heart beats. It is what we are, how we live, our thoughts, our conversations, our sight, and what we hear. It is as vital as filling our lungs with air. It is the natural result of a divine maturing process.

Do not tell Peter and John to stop being peacemakers. Oh, you can try. You can mock them, whip them, and throw them in jail. You can try to stop them. But they will respond, "We cannot help speaking about what we have seen and heard." Did God make them do it?[13] Did He force them to talk? Of course, He did not. They had become peacemakers. It was what they did. It was the natural, or should I say supernatural response to divine growth. This does not come from us. It only comes from God. It is His maturing process, not ours. It is His divine way to maturity. You see, we would not do it that way. We have not done it that

---

[13] "We cannot help speaking about what we have seen and heard." (Acts 4:20)

way. That is obvious. Maybe we can change. Maybe we can finally see how Jesus wants it done.

If this appears a little harsh, I apologize. I suppose I am speaking from my own frustration in this maturity thing. I know I am not here, but I know some who are though; men and women of God, who eat, breathe, sleep, and ooze peacemaker. I long to imitate them as they imitate Him.

Encourage Godly men and women to consider this relationship as peacemaker. Encourage men and women who do not know peace, to come to know Him.

EIGHT

The Persecuted–Attitude toward Suffering

Blessed are those who are persecuted because of righteousness, for theirs is the kingdom of heaven. Blessed are you when people insult you, persecute you and falsely say all kinds of evil against you because of me. Rejoice and be glad, because great is your reward in heaven, for in the same way they persecuted the prophets who were before you.
–MATTHEW 5:10–12

do not like to hurt. I suppose of all my pastimes, hurting is at the bottom of the list. I spend a great deal of time and resources to avoid it. TV calls me to it. Do not hurt, do this. Want to be free from pain? Try this. You know what I am talking about. You are probably a lot like me. Well, this is the part of our discussion where I have to come clean. This is hard. This is not just difficult. It is hard!

Whenever we talk of suffering, there seems to be a mystique associated with Christians that faith ends suffering. If a person has real faith, then God will relieve that person's suffering. If someone is suffering, then it is because that person has either little faith or has done something that deserves to be punished. It, unfortunately, is all over the airwaves. If you have enough faith, then God will deliver you. If He does not, then it is your fault. Claim victory. Man, that sounds good. Now, I am not trying to incite you. I just think that disciples of God who have been matured by Him have something much deeper that transcends this concept.

So here is my story and I am sticking to it. In 1988, I was painting and preaching. Yes, I was a man of the drop cloth. I was working on a job where I was painting a 110-foot tank out of a winch lift. Each time I worked my way down, I would look up at the top of the tank and see double. I went to the doctor and had some tests to see what the problem was with the double vision, but nothing definite was diagnosed. The range of double vision changed from time to time over the course of the next few years and back to the doctor I would go with a little coaxing from my wife, and nothing was determined to be seriously wrong.

I learned to live with it. It put spice in my life. If something was good, well, it was twice as good. If something was ugly, well, you know. Finally, in 1996, I got a headache that lasted three months, night and day. Then it really started to hurt. By and by with other symptoms, I ended up at a neurologist who informed me that I had multiple sclerosis. I told him that I was relieved to know it was something and that I was not just silly. He said that He did not rule out the silly; he just said I had MS.

I would like to have thought that I handled this news pretty well. I was relieved to know that it was some medical problem and not a mental deficiency. I prayed for the strength to deal with the condition. I shared the news with some individuals who were incredibly supportive and helpful. I shared the news with some people who broke badly. One brother told me that I needed to humble myself and pray to God to heal me. I told him that there was no doubt that I needed to humble myself and that I had prayed to God since 1988 to heal me. He said I needed to pray harder. We parted and I asked him to pray for me.

There is another part to this story. From 1988 to 1996, I prayed that God would take this away from me, the problems, the pain, the suffering. It never happened. In 1996, I changed my prayer. I asked God to just let me know what the problem was. In less than two weeks after I changed my prayer, I was diagnosed with MS. Now, what is the deal? Did God answer my prayers? He sure did. The first answer was no. The second one was yes. This set me on a quest. Here I am. I am a Christian. I am a minister. I want to do what God wants me to do. I want to be for Him. What am I missing? Why won't He take it away?

This quest has led me to where I am tonight. Talking to you and trying to pass on what, I believe, God has in mind for His people. I believe the thing that I was missing was a part of God's maturing process. It is the goal of maturity. It is not that I believe I am at that point, mind you. I am not. But it is the principle behind the persecuted. It is the attitude toward suffering. Many followers of God are led to believe that suffering is for the weak in faith. Many believe that the stronger you are in the faith, the more a certain spiritual immunity to suffering occurs. If suffering does occur, it is because of sin or weakness, and Satan only attacks weakness. It is like a spiritual evolutionary survival-of-the-fittest philosophy. Only the strong will survive. They are supposed to be immune from spiritual disease and physical suffering.

I have come to believe it is the opposite that is true. It is the way that maturity develops. When you become a peacemaker, you become a completely new threat to the kingdom of darkness. When you become a peacemaker, then you are now infringing on the dark side through more than just yourself. When you become a teacher, you become a target. You now have Satan's attention. He could ignore you, or he could try to quench you. He has tried to quench you from the beginning with pride, and the Lord interposed humility. He then went with contentment, and the Lord graced you with remorse for your sin. Satan tried to get you to do your own thing, but the Lord created control with you. Satan wanted you to just go through the motions, but the Lord lit the fires of desire. The devil challenged your attitudes toward others, but mercy came running. The devil tried to destroy all that was pure in your heart, but the Lord held your heart in His hand. The Deceiver tried to get you not to say a word, but the Lord stood you up to tell the world of His peace. You are now a teacher. It goes beyond, just like Job. Then Satan says,

> "Skin for skin."
> "You're gonna hurt."
> "Nip it, nip it in the bud."
> "This is it."
> "We'll see how long you stand now."
> "Bring on the rack."[14]

---

14   Peretti, Frank. Focus on the Family. Radio Broadcast, 1980-1989

Suffering has a way of putting things either in perspective or totally out of focus. There are two ways that a disciple can react, no more or no less. We either suffer and remain faithful to Him who has called us, or we suffer and give in. Jesus has led us through a remarkable growth period. It culminates with a concept that is foreign to our human ideologies. We, being human, find it difficult to understand a god who delights in the suffering of his people. This is where our logic breaks down. Our God does not delight in the suffering of His people. But our God utterly delights in the faithfulness of His children who choose to stay faithful to Him no matter what may come their way.

This is the key. If God delivers us every time we suffer, then our service will be dependent upon His relief of our suffering. The first time we suffer one second longer than we think we should, our proud, spoiled, arrogant soul will cast him off like a pair of old shoes. Our faithfulness to Him would be dependent upon our comfort, contentment, or freedom of suffering, rather than on His being God. So what He is after in our lives as His disciples is to have the kind of faith in Him that will remain faithful, no matter what happens.

Meshach, Shadrach, and Abednego were in dire circumstances (Daniel 3). They faced the mother of all furnaces. They had not yet suffered but looked into the barrel of a loaded gun with the trigger cocked. They knew it could very well be all over. They told the king something that God wanted from our lives. They said that God, whom they served, was able to deliver them from the burning fiery furnace. But if He did not, they would still not bow down and worship the ninety-foot idol of the king. This is the disciple's faith. God, whom we serve, can deliver us from anything. He can deliver us from sin, sickness, injury, persecution, disease, injustice, or anything else that you or I can imagine. He wants us to have such faith in Him that even if He does not, we will still not leave Him. This lets the plow down a little deeper. God does not want His people to suffer. He wants them to be faithful even if they do suffer. If our vision of God is for His glory, then He will be glorified in every circumstance in our lives. This is the call of the disciple. Even if you suffer, *He will still be glorified.*

Suffering is a vital ingredient to growth. It is the culmination of the maturity process. It is not the result of wickedness or lack of faith. It is the result of righteousness and mustard-seed faith. Our God is able to deliver us. We believe that. We hold that. He has proven time and time again that He can. Sometimes He will. When He does, praise God, He is glorified. Sometimes He does not though, and He is glorified even more. This is the calling. When we know He can and He does not, but we still remain faithful and confident in Him being God and glorifying Him in the midst of suffering, Satan is silenced. What else can Satan do? He has tried to make you suffer to get you to quit God. You still refuse to bow down to the idol. You have taken away Satan's power. You have multiplied God's power in your life a hundred times, and heaven is exploding with praise. God is glorified in your life by you patiently enduring suffering and staying faithful.

Now here is another aspect to this monumental climax. Peter says that Jesus suffered, leaving us an example that we should follow in His steps (1 Peter 2). Paul says that we are to become mature attaining to the whole measure of the fullness of Christ (Ephesians 4). How do we follow in His steps? How do we attain the whole measure of the fullness of Christ? It is not that we become perfect. It is not that we become sinless. That cannot be it at all. If that could be it, then He would not have had to die on the cross. It is not perfection. It is maturity, maturity to the point that we can follow His steps of suffering and still abide in Him. The Hebrews writer says that Jesus learned obedience and was made mature through suffering (Hebrews 5). Now that is something that

I cannot wrap my little mind around. I cannot grasp that concept. It is written. I believe it. It is about the Christ. If suffering played such a significant role in His life, why not mine? No matter what the circumstances, He always allows us to choose. When our faith allows us to remain loyal to Him, no matter what the suffering or persecution, then God is glorified. He then uses the faith we have to bring even more maturity. So the question of suffering is not "Why me?" The question becomes "Why not me?" So here is the crux of the matter about persecution and suffering. Suffering is something that Satan intends to turn us away from God. Satan's purpose is to hurt us so badly that we ask, "Why me?" He wants us to question God's love for us. He wants us to question our own lives. He wants us to question so that we will doubt God, think only of ourselves, and lose faith. God allows us to choose to follow.

This is not masochistic Christianity. This is not a pleasurable thing. Remember, I do not like pain. I do not like to hurt. I do not like even being uncomfortable. I have a furnace and an air conditioner in my house. Yes, even in West Virginia, we have indoor plumbing. I like to feel good physically, mentally, emotionally, and spiritually. I do many things to keep from being hurt. Yet if I am going to become mature in Jesus, I will have to suffer. Somehow, some way, I will have to suffer. It may not be one giant suffering experience. It may be a little here and a little there. It may seem that things always go wrong, and my focus gets out of kilter. But God, whom you serve, has made a promise to you. He is faithful. He will not let you be tempted above what you are able to bear (1 Corinthians 10). The Lord put Satan on a leash with Job (Job 1:12, 2:6). He said you can go this far and no farther. He does the same for you and me. Satan can only go so far. He can go no farther. What an awesome God we serve! God knows what you can take (1 Corinthians 10:13). So our suffering is directly proportional to our faith. It is not that the stronger we are in the Lord, the less suffering, and trials we have. It is the opposite. The stronger our faith, the more leash is given. That is why we praise God for our trials. That is why we count it pure joy (James 1:2–4). That is why we rejoice in our trials (Romans 5:1–5). God is still moving. He is working on me. So rejoice that your faith is such that the trials you suffer are directly proportional to your faith and you are maturing. And when the trial passes and the hurting stops, your faith has grown even more. Then the next time, the leash is let out a little further. There is always one more lesson to learn. There is always one more step to take in the direction of the suffering Christ. That is the maturing process. We go from poor in spirit to pure in heart, to suffering servant. They did it to the prophets. They did it to Jesus. Why not me?

IN BETWEEN

I would like to stop for a second and catch my breath before we go on in this little venture. After the beatitudes and just before the rest of the story, let's insert this. This is something that I believe is worthwhile. It has been helpful to me, and I hope it can be helpful to you too. The beatitudes play an important part in the realization of the rest of the story. It is from the attitudes that Jesus changes, that the remaining sermon takes its power. When the attitudes that He has changed in my life concerning God—sin, control, desire, others, the heart, salvation, and suffering—have grown, then the things that He begins to discuss become more meaningful. Each attitude of the disciple is needed in the realization of each of the remaining sections. These different sections to follow are not intended to help us develop the attitudes of the beatitudes. Instead, the attitudes of the beatitudes will help us develop these attitudes in our lives. These are the icing on the cake.

While you go through the rest of the sermon, take a little time through prayer and meditation to see the progression of the beatitudes in each section. Some may tend to lean a little more on the attitude toward God by being poor in spirit. Some may tend to emphasize mercy. One may hit home with the need for control, while another may go right to the heart of desire. Anyway, as you go through, look for the attitude of the disciple that each section needs in order for it to be absorbed as a way of life. The progression of attitudes is in each one. Every section goes from humility to suffering. They are embodied in every aspect of the remaining discussions. Yet there is one that may speak to you more than others. Look for it, and the plow will go down even deeper.

I hope that you find this refreshing. It is meant to refresh. When you read this, I hope you smile and sometimes just laugh out loud. This is burden-lifting and yoke-lightening. Our Lord wants us to enjoy serving Him and not endure it as if it is a terrible disease for being one of His followers. If I can communicate this to your heart, then our time will be well spent with the Lord's sermon. Here we go again.

Persecuted

Peacemakers

Pure in Heart

Merciful

Hunger and Thirst after Righteousness

Meek

Mourn

Poor in Spirit

NINE

Salt and Light–Attitude toward Purpose

You are the salt of the earth. But if the salt loses its saltiness, how can it be made salty again? It is no longer good for anything, except to be thrown out and trampled by men. You are the light of the world. A city on a hill cannot be hidden. Neither do people light a lamp and put it under a bowl. Instead, they put it on its stand, and it gives light to everyone in the house. In the same way, let your light shine before men, that they may see your good deeds and praise your Father in heaven.
–MATTHEW 5:13–16

One of the things that people long for each day in this society, or any other society for that matter, is purpose. In our society, millions of dollars are spent each year trying to help people find a purpose in life. As a matter of fact, millions of dollars are made each year trying to convince people that their purpose is to help them make millions of dollars. Why am I here? What am I supposed to do? Why do I exist? Of course, you know this is a big deal in our world.

Jesus knows that too. So as He continues to change and mold the attitudes of His Jewish people that He had come to be with, He helps them to understand their purpose in this universe. The illustrations that He uses are simple ones. Salt and light were common things in their world. The people on the mount were probably more attuned to the meanings of salt and light than we are today. The thing about salt and light is that both affect their environment. They influence whatever they come in contact with.

Salt affects change in a number of ways. It flavors, it preserves, and it can be used to make things better in many ways. Light does the same. It gives guidance, it gives protection, and it discovers. Well, you know how salt and light affect your world. They both can make the world a better place if they are used in the right way. But what if they lose their usefulness or do not do what they are supposed to do?

If salt no longer serves the purpose it once did, it becomes useless. If light is off or covered up, what value does it have in spreading its beams? The point is both have a purpose. If the purpose for which they are intended is not carried out, then they lose their usefulness. I am sure that anyone today can relate to this. Everyone, both believer and nonbeliever, at times feel that their lives have no purpose. The same was true in the first century. People need to know that their lives mean something. They need to know that they have a purpose. Jesus, the framer of the universe, is the only one who can show us the purpose of our lives. He takes purpose to another level. It is quite simple and obvious as well. But only He can put purpose in the proper perspective.

The purpose of God's people does not lie in the fulfillment of me. It is not by simply helping other people that I find my fulfillment. Serving is noble. Do not misunderstand. We are called as Christians to serve, but serving in and of itself is not our purpose. Serving can and oftentimes will lead to a feeling of self-worth. But do not confuse self-worth with purpose. Serving others, no matter how noble and humbling, is not the end. It is simply a means to an end.

When serving occurs as the purpose itself, then purpose becomes clouded by my sense of accomplishment in serving. I am then at a point where my delight is simply that I am a good person, and I am doing a good deed. My thought is "I must be a good person because it takes a good, humble person to do the things that I do." When that happens then serving becomes a pride thing, and those being served must show a sense of appreciation to me for what I have done for them. When the pride thing pops up, then my serving is turned into a self-righteous act that must have gratitude in order to obtain the self-worth that I desire.

Serving is why we are called. Jesus came here to serve, and we are called to follow in His steps. The attitude behind serving is what gives purpose to God's believers. The end result is to glorify God. That is the purpose of God's people, His glory. Serving is the means and God's glory is the end. This takes the attitude toward purpose into a different realm. Jesus wants His people to influence their environment. He wants His people to affect change around them. He wants His people to be a preserving force in their world. He wants His people to give guidance and direction in their society. He wants His people to be salt and to be light, but He wants His people to do it because of who He is, not because of who we are!

God's glory is the reason this universe was created. A little passage in Hebrews 2:10 says, "In bringing many sons to glory, it was fitting that God, for whom and through whom everything exists, should make the author of their salvation perfect through suffering." God is the reason that everything exists! It is not *my* self-worth. It is not *my* purpose. It is not *my* agenda. It is not *my* comfort. It is not *my* pleasure. *I am not the reason* He created the universe. *He is the reason He created the universe!* This universe was created for Him, and He is the reason it exists. That is the end. Everything else is the means to that end. Salvation, redemption, love, and serving are all means to an end. The end of the matter is God's glory.

God did not create this universe for my salvation and redemption. If that is the case, then I am the central focus. He chose to save and redeem me because this creates in me wonder and awe that the Creator of the universe loves me enough to save and redeem me. But the reason He saved and redeemed me is for His glory. That makes Him the central focus. My response to His salvation and redemption is, praise God! I choose to do that. He does not compel me. He does not force me. I choose to do it. That brings even more glory to Him because I choose to do it out of the free will He placed in me.

Love is not the reason this universe was created either. Love by itself is not the end. There are people who love those who love them without a thought of God. Love is simply a means by which the Lord of all receives the glory. This is true whether we are talking about His love or our loving each other because He first loved us. That makes Him the center of why everything exists.

Serving is not the ultimate end either. Serving is a means

by which God receives glory. That is the point of what Jesus is saying. When we serve, we are serving for the purpose of giving God the glory. That deemphasizes me and places the glory squarely on God. This is not a passive thing. We are not to allow others to make the assumption that the reason we do good deeds is for God's glory. We need to make sure that He is the one that gets the credit. If it were not for Him, good deeds would not happen. This is the attitude of purpose. God is being glorified.

It changes everything. This gives a purpose for living. It puts the entire context of our existence on a higher plane. Simple, plain, and mundane things that occur in our lives are now seen in a different way. Changing dirty diapers or mowing yards are holy things that give glory to God. Washing dishes or washing the car is viewed differently in view of the glory to God. A kind word or a hug around the neck becomes purposeful for God's glory. They are not seen as things that are useless or mundane anymore but rather as things that are purposeful.

I know a man who worked as a painter by trade. One time he was working on an apartment complex with several other painters. During the course of a few months and many hours of work, they became close enough to talk about things other than weather and football. They knew that he was a minister, and they found themselves talking about spiritual things from time to time. One day as they neared the end of the project, a few of them were working in one apartment, talking about different things. Then one young man popped a question for discussion that caught some off guard. He went through each one there and specifically asked them by name, "What is your purpose in life?" One answered that his purpose was to make as much money as he could possibly make. One said that he wanted to have as many women as he could. Another said that he really did not have a purpose but just went with the flow. The minister was the last one to be asked.

When the young man asked him the question, everyone stopped what they were doing. Brushes were wiped and hanging on their hooks. Rollers were hung in buckets. Everyone looked straight at him. He turned around and said, "My purpose in life is to glorify God." Then he had the opportunity to tell them not only about God but also about Jesus's death on the cross and what that meant to him and for them. It lasted about fifteen minutes. It was a holy time. They should have taken off their shoes. These painters who had not darkened the door of a church building in years or had no regard for God in their lives were hearing about God, who loved them more than they loved themselves. He did not know the impact it had on them, but he knew the impact it had on him. He would never forget that moment in time.

Purpose is a powerful thing. It can take a life from the realm of routine into the realm of meaning. Jesus wants us to have purpose that gives meaning to wandering hearts and lives that search for meaning. That purpose is an attitude that changes actions. That purpose is to glorify God. That purpose will allow us to love and serve others without regard to how they respond. If they are grateful for our service, it is directed toward God. If they are appreciative of our love, it is directed toward God. If, on the other hand, they are not appreciative or grateful, we still are able to accomplish our purpose in our hearts and continue to love and serve them and others. We still believe and are convinced that God gets the glory for what has been done. We know that He is the reason that we are loving and serving. It is for His glory that we are salt and light, and it gives us a reason to get up in the morning. It gives us a living, breathing reason for existence. We do not have to do something that will make the nightly news. We are doing something far greater. We are glorifying the God of the entire universe. That is why we were made. "So … whatever you do, do it all for the glory of God" (1 Corinthians 10:31).

TEN

Surpassing Righteousness– Attitude toward Motivation

Do not think that I have come to abolish the Law or the Prophets; I have not come to abolish them but to fulfill them. I tell you the truth, until heaven and earth disappear, not the smallest letter, not the least stroke of a pen, will by any means disappear from the Law until everything is accomplished. Anyone who breaks one of the least of these commandments and teaches others to do the same will be called least in the kingdom of heaven, but whoever practices and teaches these commands will be called great in the kingdom of heaven. For I tell you that unless your righteousness surpasses that of the Pharisees and the teachers of the law, you will certainly not enter the kingdom of heaven.
–MATTHEW 5:17–20

When the Lord made man in the beginning, it must have been something supremely special. God made a creation out of clay and then took His image and delicately placed it within those bones and flesh. The angels must have stood in awe. What a chance God was taking! He was creating something in His image that He was allowing outside of His total control. Oh, He could control Adam, but God in His infinite wisdom chose not to hold the reins. This new world still dripping with the wetness of beginning was set. Everything had a place and a purpose. Everything was subject to the words of the One who set it in motion. Everything was so concrete. But He chose to make Adam different. He made man with a choice. God allowed Himself to be vulnerable when He made Adam. He allowed His man to either choose Him or reject Him. But God kept a part attached to Him like a delicate string. It was like a spiritual umbilical cord. It was called His image. It was a different attachment from everything else He had made. Solomon said it like this: "He has also set eternity in the hearts of men" (Ecclesiastes 3:11). This image of God set in the hearts of individuals has a draw. It has a spiritual magnetism that drew Adam, and the people who followed, to the Creator.

In this attraction to the Creator, the image of God within man causes something inside to want to do what is right. I know that human nature does not. It is not *that* human nature about which I am talking. The human Adam, of course, chose against God as every other human, except Jesus, has done and still does. But there is a thread in every human that is attached to God by His nature that, no matter how strong or weak the urge, wants to do what is right. The great battle is between these two urges. The question becomes "How do I spark this urge to please God in my life? How do I prod this desire born of the image of God in me to foster doing what is right?"

When Jesus sat down there on the mount, he looked into the eyes of people who longed for righteousness. He knew what they longed for. They were obviously looking for something, or else they would not have made the journey to hear the Master's words. He was able, like He did with Nicodemus, (John 2:25–3:21) to look right through their eyes into the heart. All they knew of righteousness was what they had seen. The scribes and Pharisees loved to show everyone what righteousness was. They delighted in it. They basked in it. They strutted their stuff. But the folks on the mount knew this could not be the thing they longed for. Jesus knew that too. So He began where they were and started forming something that set the tone for the rest of what He had to say that day. Jesus began molding the attitude of motivation. He touched the spark of the image to help them want to have something more than what they had seen in the Pharisees.

He talked about what they knew. His people held the law and the prophets in the highest esteem. That is what they were supposed to do. He reached out and gently touched that cord that He had placed within them. He reassured them. He wanted them to know the integrity that He held in the rightness of the law and the prophets. He wanted them to know that no matter how radically, how differently He taught, He was not coming to take the law away. Jesus did not come for that purpose. Jesus came to show them what righteousness really was. He came to show them that God was right, and He gave a law that was right. Jesus was not going to do away with what was right. He was going to show them how right it was by fulfilling it.

He told them that if they broke the law or even taught someone to break the law, they were least in the kingdom of heaven. But if they kept the law and taught others to keep the law, they were great in the kingdom. I am sure there were mixed emotions here. There were probably some whose hearts sunk just a little. They knew who they were. They knew how they lived. They knew what they had seen of the law and the prophets. Their minds flew to the Pharisees. This was their idea of the law and the prophets: flowing robes, long prayers, blowing trumpets on street corners, tithing spices, and pointing fingers. They were afraid of that kind of law and prophets. They were afraid of becoming that kind of law and prophets. Then Jesus changed gears on them. The holiness of God's righteousness could never be embodied like what they knew. It had to be something different. It could not be what the Pharisees were showing.

Jesus wanted them to know that it was not like what they knew. This righteousness of God revealed to them by the law and the prophets was not what the Pharisees were living. Whew, what a relief. Jesus wanted them to know that the righteousness of the Pharisees was not what it was cracked up to be. They had a different kind of righteousness. It was self-righteousness. It was a rightness that was for people to see. Their righteousness was from the teeth out. It was a reputation righteousness. Reputation is what men think you are. The rightness of the Pharisees was only good for what people thought they were. It was to impress. It was a righteousness that was only good when people were watching. Their motivation was what others were thinking of them. They did their thing for men to see. Jesus had their attention. He exposed the motive.

Jesus with masterful explanation showed them something they were longing for. He showed them that the righteousness He wanted was a surpassing righteousness. God wants righteousness for Him. This is what surpassing righteousness is. It was different. It required character. He tugged at the string attached to the image of God in them. It called to their hearts about what God wants rather than what men see. It was a rightness that involved character. Character deals with what God knows. Character is what God knows you are. It appeals to the cord that is tied to Him, set in our hearts. It is that part of us that wants to do what God wants because it pleases Him. It is *the* motivation that cannot come from the outside. It cannot be forced. It cannot be manipulated. It cannot be coerced. It has to come from within. It comes from the God place in each of us, His nature/His image. That is the kind of righteousness that wants to do what is right, even when no one else is watching. In the wee hours of the morning, it chooses God. In the middle of a crowd, it pursues right. It is not something that is turned on and off like a light. It is a fire. It is a flame. It is the burning in the soul of Jeremiah. It is the gleam in the eye of Peter. It is the love that compelled Paul. It is the same thing that urged David. It is God in you. It is the relationship with God that wants to please Him so much that it does not matter who is watching or not watching, doing right is what is right. It is based on truth. It is based on honor. It is based on God.

Jesus touched, tugged, and now He holds that cord in His hand as He explains that this surpassing righteousness is different. They must be different. I must be different. This takes my thought of God and righteousness to a new plane. This gives me something that I need. That need in my life is motivation. The want is there. It has been there all along. God put it there with His image. Anything about God's nature is desirous of righteousness. The desire for doing and being right comes from Him. So Jesus connects the motivation for doing right to the one whose nature has been inside all along. God becomes my motivation for personal righteousness. Personal righteousness is not self-righteousness. They are two completely different entities. This personal, surpassing righteousness that Jesus calls us to is what sets the tone for the rest of the sermon. If we only follow His directives to make people think we are pretty good joes, then we are missing our calling. If we follow His directives because of who

God is, then we are catching a glimpse of what He really wants for us in our lives. We are tapping into His nature. We are calling on Him for our motivation. God is the motivation for my following Him. It is not a pat on the back. It is not a kind word in the bulletin. It is God. He knows, and that is all I need to know.

This is big stuff. It transcends things that I have come to depend on. It allows me to love, serve, give, honor, respect, encourage, change, or any other quality without the need of a response from others or by others. It allows me to be free to do what is right because of God. I have no need to be concerned about how this looks. I do not have to worry about what others think. I feel no threat about appearances. This is what allowed Jesus to eat with publicans and those thought to be judgmental. It gave Him the freedom to have his feet washed by the tears of a sinner. It compelled Him to touch lepers. He did it because it was right. He did it because of God. He did it because righteousness was personal. He embodied it. He did not do these things because people expected Him to do it. Jesus explained righteousness not because of other people, but in spite of them. This is His call to us. He is calling us to do the right thing. He is informing us to be conformed to right because His image is transforming us. There is the motivation of personal righteousness. The image of God that was set in my heart from the moment of conception becomes paramount. He tugs at that string. Oh, there is a conflict. There is a battle. It still goes on. Nature wars against nature (Romans 7:14–25). Human always conflicts with the divine.

Here is something that makes this even more complete. When we become followers of the Lord Jesus, He does something that is far wiser than anyone could have comprehended. He unites His image with His Spirit in our lives. When we give our lives to Him, when we surrender, He cleanses this vessel and then lives in it. When His image in us, given at birth, is united with His Spirit, given at rebirth, we become complete. Paul calls it "created in Christ Jesus" (Ephesians 2:10). He also calls it "a new creation" (2 Corinthians 5:17). Paul calls it "a new life" (Romans 6:4). It is God in us that helps us overcome the conflict with the human nature in us. This is where the uniting takes place and we become whole.

Yet this is the point where that marvelous choice comes into play. That point in creation where God allowed Himself to become vulnerable by making this thing called choice, now has shown Himself to be even "more" omniscient. He calls us by His nature to motivate us to choose Him. He beckons us from that part of Him in us, to do what His nature is. That spark is in each of us to do what is right. His nature in us is what causes that spark to become a fire. That fire on the inside is what Jesus is stoking in our hearts. He is creating an intense desire by His personal nature in our personal lives to become personal with Him. When that happens, external motivation is unnecessary. Many sermons will have to change. There will be no need for them. Reminders to read and study will be redundant. Serving and loving will be a way of life. Our motivation for all these things will not be because we are duty bound to do these things. It will not be for others to see. It will not be a motivation spurred by reputation righteousness that is quietly tucked away until it is needed to impress someone again. It will be a surpassing righteousness that does what is right because of God. When everything is said and done, this will be the motivation. This personal righteousness will simply motivate me to do what is right because He is my motivation for doing right. Lord, help me to understand!

ELEVEN

Anger and the Altar–
Attitude toward Relationships

You have heard that it was said to the people long ago, "Do not murder, and anyone who murders will be subject to judgment." But I tell you that anyone who is angry with his brother will be subject to judgment. Again, anyone who says to his brother, "Raca," is answerable to the Sanhedrin. But anyone who says, "You fool!" will be in danger of the fire of hell. Therefore, if you are offering your gift at the altar and there remember that your brother has something against you, leave your gift there in front of the altar. First go and be reconciled to your brother; then come and offer your gift. Settle matters quickly with your adversary who is taking you to court. Do it while you are still with him on the way, or he may hand you over to the judge, and the judge may hand you over to the officer, and you may be thrown into prison. I tell you the truth, you will not get out until you have paid the last penny.
–MATTHEW 5:21–26

t overwhelms me how much the Lord influences the believer's life. He is involved in every aspect. He is there in the quiet time. When just you and He are alone, it is awesome. When you are by yourself in the car or sitting on the porch, there is holy time between you and God. I do not know about you, but for me, those times are not too often. They are usually too few for my own good. Most of my time is not alone because I am not alone in this world. There are a couple of billion of us walking around here on this little planet, and because of that, we are together. Here is where I find most of my problems. It is not that others are the problem. It is that I must relate in some way to them. I must interact with them. On the phone, at the stoplight, at work, at school, at church, in line at the grocery store, at the game: I must rub elbows with other people. How I relate to those folks becomes a major thing. Relationships come in all sizes and shapes. They are like the kids who like hot dogs: fat ones, skinny ones, ones that climb on rocks, tough ones, sissy ones, and even some with chicken pox. Good relationships are the ones I like. I like the Al Dunkleman relationships. I like the Tom Racer relationships. I really like the one-of-a-kind Brenda Matthews relationship. Yes, we all work at these relationships. We nurture them. We foster them. We do things that hurt each other, but with both of us working on them, they work. I like them because they are easy to like. They respond. You know exactly what I am talking about.

It is the other relationships that give me the problem. The relationships that do not respond the way I want are the ones that strain the soul. These, unfortunately, are the ones that take up the majority of my life. They are the ones that Jesus talks about in the next point of His sermon. The Father influences the way we relate to others with the rough, distant, and undependable relationships just as much as He does the soothing, close, dependable ones. He is and wants to be involved in these ties too.

Jesus has already told the crowd that He is *for* the law and the prophets. He has told them that the law is needful and necessary. Yet now He begins a journey to take them beyond. He raises the bar. The baseline of the law was good. It affected how they lived. It affected how they raised their children. It touched their in-laws. It molded the way they dealt with their friends. It shaped the way they dealt with their adversaries. It was the standard of living. Jesus uses the law to take them to a higher standard. This standard changes everything because He has involved God to a greater degree. The image of God in them puts things in a different perspective. God is not just in them alone. His image is in everyone. His image is in mom and dad. His image is in their husbands and wives. His image is stored in their children. But His image is in their adversaries as well. The ones who oppose them, however unthinkable, bear the image of God. So how does the Lord of the universe communicate this concept? He draws a comparison.

The comparison is "You have heard ... but I tell you." You have heard this. Where did they hear it? It was the baseline. It was the law. It was the standard of living. This was not unfamiliar territory. The synagogues were full of it. The temple teaching demanded it. The Pharisees proclaimed it. Jesus even said it. But Jesus said more! He raises the standard of conduct by changing the attitude of the hearer. He brings the Lord of glory into the discussion. By His comparisons, He equates things by their judgments. Murder brought judgment. That was the baseline. Jesus says that anger is the equivalent of murder because both produce the same judgment. *Raca*, a term of contempt, makes one answerable to the Sanhedrin. *Fool*, a term of equal contempt, makes the consequence far more than a slap on the wrist by a council. Jesus says it is a hell-bound offense. So, what *is* Jesus saying? He has taken physical things and elevated them into spiritual terms.

He has taken things that they took for granted, meant nothing, and elevated them to a different level. The reason that anger and contempt for people are as bad as or worse than anything physical is because of one thing. That one thing is the treatment of the image of God in them.

The attitude toward relationships with people is based on the esteem we have for the image of God in them. God is in the middle of everything. He is the one who loves the unlovable. How does He do it? He does it because even the unlovable bear His image. He made them for Him. He can treat both the saved and the sinner with love and compassion. He can ask for forgiveness for even nail-driving soldiers. It is a level that goes beyond the baseline. It stems from God. Our relationship with others is based on our relationship with God. He is the reason that we are able to respond to opposition without anger. He is the reason that even though the actions may indeed seem foolish, the actor is not a fool. He is the reason we get along with each other. Pride is not involved. Standing up for myself is not in the equation. My feelings, my thoughts, and my formal announcements to a brother of his misunderstanding are not the necessary things. The necessary things relate to my brother because of whose image is in him.

Then Jesus puts all this into another perspective. He takes relationships with people and puts God in the picture. My relationship with God is related to my brother. Worship is the ultimate in the God relationship. Sacrifice, forgiveness, and confession are all a part of the worship experience. Offering a gift at the altar brought all this to their minds. Worship was the thing that Jews cherished. They traveled to worship. They sacrificed many things to worship. They came to the temple to worship, often. Jesus now was telling them, "There is a problem." Their worship to God is directly affected by relationships with each other. This is an attention-getter. Well, it gets my attention anyway.

Here, the level of what Jesus teaches becomes more involved. It is not eliminating the law. He did not come to abolish the law. He came to take the standard and raise it. It is raising the level of conduct to a higher, nobler plane. He elevates the relationships that we have with men and women to the holiness of worship. One is predicated on the other. I always wanted to keep my worship between God and me. It is a personal thing. Worship is individual. Indeed, it is individual, but life is not. God is not, and God's image in men is not. So God does not want us to try and warm-fuzzy Him with sacrifices asking for forgiveness, praising Him for His wonder when I have just torn the heart out of my brother. Think of how this really is. God knows our hearts. He knows our relationships. He knows what we think and how we act. When we are on the outs with people, fiercely at odds with others and then we come to offer our gift at the altar, who is being impressed? It is almost like God does not know about what is happening with my brother. It is like God only knows what everybody else knows. So I present my gift, confess over the sacrifice, and offer the fellowship offering. I stick my thumbs under my suspenders and think how wonderful it is to worship God. That may sound a little petty, but really it is what I do. I make it look good. Everyone thinks it looks good. Everyone likes worship. Everyone thinks it looks and sounds good but the one whose heart is breaking because I abused His image in my brother.

Jesus now supplies grace in the midst of this realized misery. He supplies a way of escape. He always does. He promised He would. The way of escape is to go to the brother and make things right. Does it sound tough? If the beatitudes are being formed in our lives, it will not be as tough. Pride will not stop us because humility is the rule now. Sin will not stop me because I know I am in the same boat as he is. Meekness helps too. It allows me to be in control. Hunger and thirsting come into play because of this disciple's desire to do right. Mercy may be a big deal here. If I need to be merciful, I can because of the mercy that I have received. "Pure in heart" is a big one because I may have to backtrack a bit when I find out how I need to reconcile with my brother.

The beauty of it all is that two things occur. I am reconciled with my brother, and I can worship God. I want this to be in my life. I want to be able to do this in my life. I want relationships with people, and I want a relationship with God that enhances my relationship with people. Jesus gives me a way to do both. It will take a change of attitude before the action ever happens. The attitude is toward relationships. God must be the one who effects and affects everything.

Jesus adds one more little tidbit into this equation: the idea of consequences. Ouch! I could have gone all day without hearing that. You see, there is a definite reason for settling matters quickly. It surely has to do with my relationship with God, but there is a short-term matter as well. What if I am so wrong that it takes me to jail? Jesus assures us that no matter what the spiritual end, there will be consequences for our actions as well. This is a thing that our society needs to hear. Actions do produce consequences. Our children need to hear it. Our employees need to hear it. Our employers need to hear it. Our elected representatives need to hear it. Judges, lawyers, doctors, ministers, teachers, butlers, bakers, and candlestick makers all need to be made aware of the fact that there really are consequences to our actions.

Two things that are really important come from this section. Relationships are crucial and consequences will come. So maybe keep in mind the way you deal with people. Try to view the nature that has been placed within the people you come in contact with. It may really have an effect on relating to God and to them. Do not let anger alter your altar.

TWELVE

The Hand and the Eye–
Attitude toward Temptation

You have heard that it was said, "Do not commit adultery." But I tell you that anyone who looks at a woman lustfully has already committed adultery with her in his heart. If your right eye causes you to sin, gouge it out and throw it away. It is better for you to lose one part of your body than for your whole body to be thrown into hell. And if your right hand causes you to sin, cut it off and throw it away. It is better for you to lose one part of your body than for your whole body to go into hell. –MATTHEW 5:27–30

This is probably one of the more difficult sections for me in the sermon. It is not because of the subject so much as what He said about the subject. There could be a literal understanding of this section. Heaven and hell are too real to just ignore it. Going to heaven is more important than any eye or any hand. If I had the choice one second after death as to whether I could go to heaven maimed or go to hell with everything intact, I would choose the former. Yet I do not believe that Jesus is talking in literal terms. I believe Jesus is using these radical terms to speak to covenant children of God about something that affects every believer.

There is one thing that is common to those who heard the words of Jesus on that mountain and the one who reads the words that were spoken on that mountain. The common element that involves both of us is temptation. It is a universal thing. It is not common in the sense that I take it for granted. It is common because we both share them. Temptations are a part of the believer's life. It is Satan's way of trying to get me back. He is masterful in the art. He has perfected it. He tries any temptation he can to entice me to be drawn away from the one who loves me. To be tempted is not wrong. Jesus was tempted from the wilderness to the garden to the cross. So I must assume that if He was tempted, I will be too. If I am tempted, it is not a weakness of faith. It is a strategy of Satan to deceive me. Temptations become wrong when I give in to them. They are no longer temptations then; they become sin (James 1:13–15). So what do I need to understand about temptation?

I suppose it is proper that Jesus uses an illustration of a temptation that any red-blooded male can relate to. He made me with passion and desires. His divine decrees tell me how to fulfill these God-given desires (Hebrews 13:4). He also now warns me that Satan knows these passions and desires and will use them to tempt me to give in, in a way to cause me to sin. Sexual sins are sometimes exceedingly difficult to talk about. It is kind of a taboo thing to talk about where I come from. Oh, we touch on it now and then, but it brings a bit of a red face and discomfort in the tone of voice. Jesus had no qualms about facing this tough problem in His sermon. He wanted to deal with these passions right at the beginning. After all, it affects everyone on the planet. God did not create Adam and Eve neuter. He made male and female. So because of who we are, Jesus dealt with it.

Obviously, the folks on the mount were just about like me. They had problems with situations that involved these sexual ideas just like our society does. Satan used their passions to tempt them just like he uses my passions to tempt me. The key here is how do I deal with these temptations? Jesus did not want them to simply keep the standard of action that they were accustomed to. Jesus again uses comparison to equate two different things. His comparison is adultery to lustfully looking at a woman. Adultery is a physical thing. It requires two people doing an unholy action. They knew what it was and the consequences. But Jesus again raises the bar. He equates the physical, concrete thing called adultery with a spiritual, intangible thing called lust. He does not intend to minimize adultery in any way. What Jesus does is maximize what already exists in the heart. Before any action happens, the heart is involved. The thought of the heart precedes any action. It is thought about. It is visualized. Jesus equates looking at a woman to lust after her with adultery. This was radical. It took something that most were not involved with and exposed it as something that anyone could be involved with because of the heart.

The idea in this illustration is that both adultery and lust are the same heart condition. Both are sins. Since both are sins, both have the same consequences. The problem here is that the look implicates the heart. When the heart is implicated, the actions are too. The idea is what is wanted by the one who looks. Jesus is trying to help us to understand that there is an attitude toward temptation that He wants fostered. That attitude is to try to eliminate situations that cause temptation. There are two options here. We can either change the look or change the heart that causes the look.

Jesus then calls on two situations that are very outlandish. He says that if your eye causes you to sin, gouge it out and throw it away. Then He says that if your hand causes you to sin, cut it off and throw it away. Now is Jesus saying to literally gouge out your eye or cut off your hand? That could be it. If we consider the wonder of heaven and the torment of hell, either would be worth the cost. But I do not believe that is the real lesson. The reason I believe this is because if one eye looks lustfully, the other one will too. If one hand practices sin, the other will too. The problem is not the eye or the hand. The problem is the heart that controls the eye and the hand. The heart is what Jesus is dealing with. It is the heart that wants to look lustfully. It is the heart that puts itself in a situation that has the opportunity to look lustfully. It is the heart that willingly—yes, willingly—attempts to look with the intent of lust.

This may sound a little coarse and rough. It is coarse and rough, but it is true. The heart that wants to look lustfully will put itself in a situation that, although it may not be willing to do the action, is willing to do the look with the thought of the action. After all, who would know? Who would know what a good man, a believer in God is thinking? No one would imagine a covenant child of God would think it. No one would know that he looked and desired. No one would know but him and God. This is the point that the bar is raised. Jesus is trying to develop disciples who have that inward personal righteousness, who want to refrain from looking because they want to please God. This is that surpassing righteousness that is based on who God is rather than what others think.

The question here is what causes the look? A heart that *wants to do* what *it wants to do* causes the lustful look. It stems from pride. Pride is the conflict in the heart that prevents submission to the will of God. Pride of the heart attempts to satisfy the passions that God built within me in ways that I desire rather than allowing those passions to be satisfied by God's will for me. Pride is the thing that causes me to willingly allow myself access to places, situations, and things where the temptation to look is fostered. Pride of the heart desires my satisfaction, my enjoyment, and my passions rather than pleasing God.

So what is the solution that Jesus poses to this prolific question? Jesus says that it is better to go to heaven with one eye than to go to hell with two good eyes. Jesus says that it is better to go to heaven with one hand than to go to hell with my whole body intact. Is Jesus talking about literal eyes and hands? I do not think so. He is talking about situations. Gouging out eyes and cutting off hands do not correct the heart condition. The answer is changing the heart and changing the situation. The eye and the hand are not the problem. The problem is the situation that the heart allows the eye and the hand to be involved in. Jesus wants us to change the situation that causes the temptation. Jesus wants us to have a heart that wants to remove itself or stay away from a situation that will cause temptation. His application of the truth is that if a situation causes a problem with temptation, change the situation. The eye that causes me to sin is like that situation that causes me temptation. Change that situation. He wants me to be willing to "cut it off" and "throw it away" from me. Get rid of that situation that causes temptation. The hand that causes me to sin is like that situation that causes me temptation. Change the situation.

94

Cut it off and throw it away. Get rid of that situation that causes temptation.

Oh, this takes meekness. This takes control that is consistent with a maturing disciple. It takes a heart that has been trained by the trainer to long for righteousness. It comes from a heart that is bent on pleasing the one whose image lives within him. This is not just for sins that attract me in a sexual way. It is for any attractive sin. Any attractive temptation that will lead me into sin will fall under this get-away-from-it approach.

Now, I am not naive enough to think that we can get away from everything that Satan throws at us, or we can eliminate every temptation he puts in our path. Even monasteries cannot isolate enough for that. But I am truthful enough to know that there are situations and places that I can refrain from to eliminate some temptations. There are circumstances that I can change to keep conversations holy. There are sights that I can refuse to view that will nip temptation in the bud. There are situations that I can revise or eliminate to keep associations on a righteous plane. I realize that I do not control temptations. Satan does. He slips around; like the roaring lion, he is trying to devour me. I know that. He blindsides me all the time. I cannot control him. But I can try to control me. I can try to control my heart. I can nurture a heart that wants to do God's will in my life and can control some situations that deal with some temptations.

The purpose here is not that we can eliminate all situations that cause temptations. That is impossible because of the ruler of this dark world. The *key* is to have a heart that seeks to do what God wants and not what I want. I want to do my best not to get into slippery situations that cause slipping. The bottom line here is that the attitude toward temptation is one that we try to avoid because we want to. It stems from a heart that loves the Father and seeks to please Him in what we see and do. The heart of the matter of the eye and the hand is the heart that wills and wants to follow the Father. It is the heart that directs the eyes and the hands into His will because the eye and the hand will always do what the heart wants. May the Lord bless our hearts in everything we see and do.

THIRTEEN

The Marriage Affair–
Attitude toward Faithfulness

It has been said, "Anyone who divorces his wife must give her a certificate of divorce." But I tell you that anyone who divorces his wife, except for marital unfaithfulness, causes her to become an adulteress, and anyone who marries the divorced woman commits adultery.
–MATTHEW 5:31–32

The politicians acknowledge it. Society ponders it. Families suffer through it. It is a breakdown. It seems that everybody knows about it. Everyone opposes it. But it still goes on. The failure to esteem the sanctity of marriage has affected families, communities, and nations and has to be one of the greatest problems of this generation. It is not something new. It was a problem on the mount as well. It was a problem among covenant children of God. It was to the Jews that Jesus was speaking. Maybe there *is* more to this little section than just an argument on marriage, divorce, and remarriage. Maybe Jesus is addressing something that is more than just an issue in churches. Maybe Jesus is letting the plow down to help us see that the problem is not just divorce. The underlying issue is faithfulness. That is the attitude that Jesus is addressing. Jesus wants His disciples to have faithfulness in every aspect of their lives.

Jesus is making a comparison again, and this time, divorce is in the middle of it. The comparison is divorce for any reason versus divorce for unfaithfulness. The first was the standard that they knew. All that was needed to terminate a marriage was a certificate of divorce. Notice that the Lord is not speaking to women. He is speaking to men. There is no mention of the woman's plight toward a man. Jesus is very sternly talking to men who were taught by tradition and teachers of the law that women were, in their view, no more than a paper towel. They were disposable. They could divorce their wives for any reason. Think about it. They could pack her bags for any reason. You name it. Burn the bread and she could be gone. Now, we are talking about any reason. This may be a little extreme, but it could have been true. It could have been anything. The thing that amazes me is that these were God's people, and they were ending something that was as old as creation. Two people created in God's image who had pledged themselves to each other could be divorced for any reason.

The implications of this thought in the Jewish tradition were that women were of little value. Women were not worth a lifetime of commitment. This was an excuse rather than a reason. This certificate of divorce only gave the opportunity of termination to men. There was no mention of women being granted this luxury of selfishness and pride. But Jesus sternly says to the men who are listening that divorce is not for any reason. Divorce for God's people can be caused only by unfaithfulness. Jesus is giving directives for God's people, yet He implies something that I believe has been missed. He implies that divorce for any other reason is an injustice for the woman. He wants them to know that God's image was in Eve as well as Adam. Wives are worth a lifetime commitment. Jesus raises the value and sanctity of wives to a level that they had not known.

In their world, the commitment of the husband was not the central issue. Jesus now shows them that the husband's commitment to the wife is the central issue. That commitment to the marriage of a man and a woman was supreme. It was not to end for any reason. The marriage was to be held in high esteem. Jesus is telling them that marriage is made up of forgiveness, forbearance, and mercy. If there was a problem between the covenant husband and the covenant wife, forgive, forbear, and be merciful like God does and is to you. That is the implication that is painted all over this passage. That is what disciples do.

This is an extraordinary teaching to these folks. It really hits the men hard. Of course, they needed to be. The results of their actions for any reason did not affect them. It only affected the women. When the man divorced the woman for any reason, it made her an adulteress. It not only made her an adulteress, but it made anyone who married her commit adultery. What able-bodied, godly Jewish man would marry a woman who was an adulteress? It punished the wife. The man who divorced her for any reason assumed no responsibility whatsoever. That practice punished the woman for the man's lack of commitment to her.

Jesus is trying to help them understand that marriage is sacred. It is holy. It is good. It was intended by God to fulfill the passions and desires that He placed within them. It is meant to last a lifetime, and faithfulness to that lifetime commitment is the central issue. Here we go again. The heart is the key. If faithfulness is embedded in the heart, then any reason will not exist. Faithfulness to the marriage is the thing the Lord is teaching men who did not see faithfulness as important. The reason that we know that faithfulness is an important issue is because unfaithfulness is the only reason that a marriage can end in divorce. I did not say it. Jesus did. For His people who believe in Him, He lifts the standard of marriage to an all-time high.

He wants disciples who are faithful to Him and partners who are faithful to each other because of their faithfulness to Him. When this happens, marriage will last a lifetime. When this happens, the station of women will be elevated to new heights. When this happens, the relationship will become equal between the two. When disciples of the Lord claim Him as Lord, their relationship will be the beneficiary. This is the point. The Lord is in the middle of everything in my life and every relationship. It stems from my value of Him in my heart that then affects every other relationship in my life.

It is in this relationship that I must learn to apply my maturity in Christ as a believer. To most, this is not a problem. To most covenant children of God, this relationship with Christ causes their marriage relationship to flourish. To most believers, this is a way of life because of the Lord. But to some, this relationship is somewhat similar to worship. It is viewed as a personal, individual thing. It is taken for granted. It is assumed that the partner in marriage is common. Things happen. Personalities are rubbed the wrong way. Feelings are hurt. Anger is stirred. Love is replaced with tolerance. Tolerance becomes strained. Two disciples who claim to revere God hold each other in contempt. I do not love her anymore. I would rather not be around him. The marriage of two people who are believers is ended. I wish this were not a possible scenario. But unfortunately, it is. You know it and I know it. But it does not have to be that way.

Jesus wants His people to be devoted to Him. He wants His husbands and wives to be devoted to each other. He longs for faithfulness in His people. This faithfulness extends to every aspect of life. This is where the maturity of Jesus's disciples is shown. Unfaithfulness shows a state of the heart. It explains something about a believer. Faithfulness is based upon the choice that God placed within each person. Faithfulness is not based upon the circumstances of life. It is not something that just happens. It is not thrown into the realm of chance. It is not predicated upon what others think or even how others act. It is solely rooted in our hearts as a choice. Faithfulness is a heart choice. Faithfulness is an on-purpose thing. It is a character of the nature of God. He is faithful. He calls upon His disciples to partake of that divine nature.

When unfaithfulness occurs, it has come about because I have made a choice not to be faithful in whatever situation. Unfaithfulness shows that the heart has chosen something that conflicts with what God wants. If I choose something other than what God wants, then I have chosen something that I want. (Notice that the section on the lustful look precedes this section.) There is the pride thing again. Pride is the thing that causes me to do what I want instead of what God wants. Pride is the basis for unfaithfulness. Of course, I now have to go back to "poor in spirit," which is my view of God and who He is. I begin again. That is the beauty of serving God. He always allows us to start over. He is the God of new beginnings.

Unfaithfulness can end a marriage. Here is the beauty of serving God as a believer. It does not have to end a marriage. If unfaithfulness occurs in a marriage, the believer can maturely be merciful and forgive. What a beautiful thing mercy is. Mercy is more of a preservative than salt. Mercy will preserve even a marriage that has been dragged through the pits of unfaithfulness. The sanctity of marriage and the attitude toward faithfulness are the underlying principles of this section. It is why Jesus chose to deal with this problem in the society of the Jews in the first century. It is why I must deal with the problem in my society today. It is why Christians must deal with faithfulness in marriages every day. Faithfulness to God and to each other is a supreme thing.

FOURTEEN

Do Not Swear at All–
Attitude toward Truthfulness

Again, you have heard that it was said to the people long ago, "Do not break your oath, but keep the oaths you have made to the Lord." But I tell you, Do not swear at all: either by heaven, for it is God's throne; or by the earth, for it is His footstool; or by Jerusalem, for it is the city of the Great King. And do not swear by your head, for you cannot make even one hair white or black. Simply let your "Yes" be "Yes," and your "No," "No;" anything else beyond this comes from the evil one.
–MATTHEW 5:33–37

H e was a nice guy. He was funny. He was a hard worker. He loved his family. He had a problem. The first time I met him, he told me a lot of stories. A coworker asked if I knew him. I said that I had never met him before. The coworker told me to believe about half of what he told me. He was right. Although he was a nice guy and was devoted to his family, he had a problem with the truth. If he really wanted you to believe him, he would preface his story with "Now, I ain't a-lyin' this time." The truth is the truth is under attack from a variety of different directions, even from good people.

It is amazing how truth can be used to be deceptive. It can be manipulated. It can be cloaked. It can be untruthful. Spin is the catchword. I remember a time when spin referred to a toy top or a carnival ride. Today, spin has an altogether different meaning. Spin is the perception of truth that the individual who is speaking is using. Perception—now that is the key word. Truth in our society has taken a back seat to perception. The perception of the truth has become the norm in politics, in business, and unfortunately, in just about every aspect of life. Spin is the concept that the evening news programs use to describe what politicians want voters to believe. It is used to communicate some reports or explanations that have some elements of truth. It is not the whole truth. It is part truth and part deception. It has made truth something that causes folks to be unbelieving and apprehensive.

Truth has become a rare commodity. Evolutionists want us to believe that science is the truth. Humanists want us to believe that man is the truth. Sociologists want us to believe that situations determine the truth. The reality is that there is truth and the one who is truth revealed it. He knows more about truth than everyone in the world put together. He is the sole authority on truth. So when He speaks, I should listen.

I find myself again listening to truth speak on the mount. His sermon is now directed toward the very thing that He embodies. Deception obviously was as much in demand in the first century as it is today. It was used to manipulate a way around telling the truth, by using elements of truth as a cover. Jesus was trying to deal with the attitude toward truth when He spoke of not swearing at all. He again makes a comparison. He compares the old standard with a new standard. The old standard was to keep your oaths made to the Lord. The new and higher standard is not to swear at all. Was it right to keep my word? Was it right to carry through with a pledge? Of course, the answer is yes.

The problem with the Jews was that they used God or something in relation to God to try to deceive. They swore by heaven, earth, Jerusalem, and even by their own head in order to give credibility to what they were saying. It was like cloaking deception by an authority related to God. Then when the oath was called into question, they would "crawfish" by saying that they did not swear by God. They saw this as a way to get what they wanted without the necessity of being truthful. Jesus says for me to simply let my word stand for itself. Let your yes be yes and your no be no. That is all that is necessary if I am truthful.

What they were trying to do was relate their manipulation of the truth to some perceived authority to deceive the person they were talking to. They appealed to heaven as a perceived authority in addition to what they said to give credibility to their deception. They used the earth and Jerusalem the same way. They were trying to tie their words to the perception that if I swear by something holy, then it must be true. If I bind what I say to something related to God, then even if you may doubt just my words, you will believe me because of the perceived authority that I have used. The purpose was not to give credence to the words. It was to have wiggle room to get out of it. It was manipulating the truth for the purpose of deception. It was like crossing my fingers when I lie. I deceptively try to lie and want it to be believed as the truth without any consequences.

The fact is that the perceived authorities that they were using (heaven, earth, Jerusalem) were all related to God. Heaven, as Jesus said, is God's throne. The earth is His footstool. Jerusalem is the city of the great king (David) chosen by God as ruler. Any oath related to any one of these perceived authorities relates the deception to God's authority because of His relationship to these things. They even tried to relate an oath to their life. The relationship of swearing by my head is like saying that I would stake my life on it. The head is the essence of life. But Jesus says that life is not something to use as an authority because I have no control. I cannot even control whether my hair turns white, turns loose, or stays black.

So what is Jesus saying? Is He talking about taking the witness stand and saying I affirm instead of I swear? I do not think this is the application at all. Jesus wants his disciple to be a person of truth. He wants His people to be folks who keep their word. He wants my words to be truthful to the point that I do not have to use something else that will enhance the believability of what I say. When my truthfulness and credibility are so inconsistent that I must appeal to something else to invoke believability, it is almost like saying, "I ain't a-lyin' this time." Jesus wants His disciples to have the attitude toward truth in their hearts. Jesus wants His disciples to know that simple truth is better than an oath related to some authority for believability even if it is true.

Surrounded by Jesus's directive are some observations that are worth mentioning because they relate to truth. Half-truths are not truths at all. Half-truth implies that there is some truth in what is being said. It also implies that there is some deception in what is being said. Half-truths hold just enough truth to sound believable, but their purpose is to deceive. It is like getting a phone call and instead of taking it, I step out the door and have someone say that I just stepped out for a minute. Yes, I have stepped out. That is the truth. The deception occurs because I am here and capable of answering the phone. That may seem a bit technical and legalistic, but it is still the truth. Jesus wants His people to be upright people who delight in truth.

Truthfulness eliminates the need for something extra to force or coerce belief. That would be like an oath. If I consistently and constantly practice truthfulness, then there is no need to attach some authority to my words for backup. That is why Jesus says to just say yes or no.

Forced or coerced belief using some authority (oath) to manipulate truth is the biggest lie of all. If manipulation and deceit are the purpose of my words, then appealing to God's authority as part of the deception for the purpose of believability becomes the greatest lie of all. It is impossible for God to lie. He has no part in it. It is not truthful to try to include Him in it.

This is the point Jesus is trying to get His disciples to. He wants me to understand that my words show what is in my heart. If truth is in my heart, then it will be what is spoken. If I say untrue things and try to deceive, then untruth and deceit are in my heart already. My words are indicative of what is in my heart (Luke 6:45, see also Matthew 12:34). The heart controls. Whatever comes out of my mouth as communication had its formulation in the heart. The heart is where my words originate. My words are the pulse of my heart. My words are the show-and-tell of the heart. If I am truthful, then it is because truthfulness is in my heart. If I speak in half-truths, deception, and lies, then my heart is full of half-truths, deceptions, and lies. Jesus is developing an attitude toward truth in His disciples' hearts.

Here is a footnote to this whole discussion. My words show the value that I place on the hearer. If I speak the truth, then the hearer has great value to me. If I am willing to deceive, then I do not value the one who is hearing my words. The implication—truth and this one have little worth to me. It may not be a coincidence that Jesus placed this little section on truthfulness right after the sections on lust and adultery. There may have been questions that needed to be answered, truthfully.

So what conclusions do I draw? The conclusion of the whole matter is to be truthful. It is to have a heart that has truth living inside. When truth lives in me, then my communications with others will be truthful. I will not have to hem-haw around with half-truths and deceptions. I will not want to cloak what I say. I will not spin it. I want to be truthful and honest. It will become as natural as breathing. That is what pure hearts do. They say what is in their hearts. Lord of truth, help me to be truthful. Change my heart.

FIFTEEN

The Cheek, the Cloak, and the Kilometer–Attitude toward Surrender

You have heard that it was said, "Eye for eye, and tooth for tooth." But I tell you, do not resist an evil person. If someone strikes you on the right cheek, turn to him the other also. And if someone wants to sue you and take your tunic, let him have your cloak as well. If someone forces you to go one mile, go with him two miles. Give to the one who asks you, and do not turn away from the one who wants to borrow from you.
–MATTHEW 5:38–42

used to play softball. I played in leagues, and I also played in tournaments. I played softball in the rain. I played once trying to finish a tournament that ended in the bottom of the seventh because the fog was so thick. You could not see the outfield. The ball was hit, and it was a home run because no one knew where it went. Sometimes though, these young men who played softball could not control their pride or their tempers. Many tournaments ended in all-out brawls. Fists and bats would swing, and blood would fly. There was a friend of mine who had played softball for several years and had been a vital part of these disagreements on several occasions. He had become a Christian, and he was really trying to change. Yet his reputation preceded him. He had avoided the fisticuffs several times after his conversion. This one time, it was almost unavoidable. The fight broke out. Some guy hit him right on the side of the head. He kept his composure, and like a good man, turned the other cheek. Well, the other fellow, not being a Christian, I might add, hit him on the other cheek. My dear brother was like Popeye. He stood all he could stand, and he could not stand anymore. When the fellow hit him on the other cheek he said, "Old buddy, you've done run out of Bible," and he hit him right in the mouth.

When Jesus talked about turning the other cheek, I do not think He was legislating rules about squabbles at softball games. This was not a law governing fighting and lawsuits. This was something much deeper. It was something about an attitude of the heart. That attitude of the heart was the attitude toward surrender. It was the attitude toward submission. Submission goes directly to the core of "poor in spirit." After all, the Jews were of a certain mentality that involved equal retribution. Jesus appealed to that very mindset that they had learned. It was a way of life because it was what was commanded by the law and the prophets. His comparison again raises the standard of conduct for His believers.

Of course, the standard of conduct is changed by first changing the standard of the heart.

In this section, Jesus is trying to change the attitude toward surrender, and the thing that was directly opposed to surrender was pride. The comparison Jesus draws is an eye for an eye and a tooth for a tooth versus do not resist an evil person. The eye-for-an-eye standard was a "just" standard. It was the right of retaliation. It allowed for the defense of a person against an attack. It was the idea that good has a right to protect against evil. It also left God out of the picture. It left no room for God's vengeance. Jesus, on the other hand, was introducing a foreign concept. This concept went to the heart of retaliation. It struck at the core of why I hit back. Jesus said that his disciples should

Turn the other cheek.
Give your cloak as well.
Go the second mile.
Give and do not turn away.

All these codes of conduct were different from what they had learned. It was common practice to retaliate. A blow brought a blow. If someone sues to take away my tunic, then the tunic was all they would get. If a Roman soldier demanded I carry his load for a mile, then the mile was all he would get and not a step farther. If someone wanted to borrow from me, then that was my choice.

Jesus turned these ideas upside down. He looked at the cause of retaliation, greed, selfishness, and prejudice. The cause of each was pride. The principles of pride involve personal pronouns. *Me, mine,* and *I* are always involved in pride. Pride is the thing that causes me to want to hit back. You cannot do that to *me* and get away with it. Pride causes *me* to want to keep everything I have because it is *mine.* Pride causes *me* to do just what is required. It is all *I* have to do. It is pride that is the underlying principle behind the actions that Jesus describes. So His call to His disciples is to surrender the pride. Pride is directly opposed to "poor in spirit" because it places *me* at the center of it all. I become the reason for my existence. What I have and am willing to do is decided by what is comfortable or acceptable to me.

Pride is also the root of prejudice. Pride causes *me* not to give and to be someone who turns away. The idea is that *I* will give it but not to you. It carries with it the idea of prejudice. There are some that *I* would be willing to give to but not to those who do not meet *my* standard of charity. Pride is the source of this type of prejudice. Jesus is elevating the standard of conduct by eliminating the source of the thing that prevents it: pride.

The opposite of pride is humility. It takes a humble heart to follow Jesus. These things seem very demanding to *my* proud heart. They seem unreasonable to the pride that swells up in *me*. That is why in order for submission to Jesus to occur, humility is the starting point. It takes being poor in spirit in order to submit. The submission to Jesus is predicated on humility. So with that in mind, let's look at some of the principles of surrender.

Surrender of pride allows *me* to leave some room for the vengeance of God. I am not talking just when someone smacks me in the face. *I* am talking anytime someone does wrong or performs an injustice toward *me*. This could be a slanderous remark. It could be a slur to my character. It could be just about anything that would cause *me* to want to hit back or retaliate in some way. Jesus is calling His disciples to a higher standard. That standard allows room for God in His infinite wisdom to do the vindicating. Now, it may not happen in this life, but rest assured, God is the ultimate when it comes to vengeance. He can do it much better than you or me (Romans 12:19). This involves Him and His wisdom. Remember, even the person who attacks has someone's image in him or her. God is the one who is able, in justice, to deliver retribution. So we are called to surrender the pride that would cause us to take vengeance or retaliation into our own hands. Leave room for God to work His will in the life of the attacker.

Surrender of pride also allows me to realize that everything I have comes from God anyway. Pride is a precarious thing. It causes me to place too much emphasis on my accomplishments. It causes me to think that whatever I have obtained came by my hand and by my work. It leaves God out of the picture. If I surrender my pride, when it comes to my possessions, then I am not as attached to them. I realize that the Lord gives, and the Lord takes away. Blessed be the name of the Lord (Job 1:21). Pride wants to hold and hoard. It brings greed. Greed is very sticky. It clings to whatever it touches. Surrender of this in my life will trust God for what we need. It allows our possessions to be as fluid as the stock market, knowing that God is the supplier of our needs.

Just getting by is a concept that has been cultivated by pride as well. It is rooted in selfishness. Surrender of that pride allows me to be able to do a little extra. It allows me to be able to do more than what is required of me. Pride is in direct conflict with the second mile. Pride produces selfishness that does just enough because that is all that is required of me. I am the center of selfishness. My wants and desires, my comfort and convenience are the ultimate concern. Surrendering this selfish pride frees me to go beyond the bounds of selfishness because I am no longer the concern. I can interpose God's glory into the situation. The reason I continue to go the second mile is for His glory, not my ease.

Surrender of pride also allows me to overcome prejudice. It allows me to help meet the needs of anyone who may have a need and who asks me for help. It takes no thought of how deserving this person is. It takes no thought of who the person is. It is not a mindset that demands a standard of criteria to be met before help can be given. Pride is the thing that demands a standard to be met. It takes the form of prejudice. Surrender knows no limits to the person who is being helped. Surrender does not require my standards to be placed on their need. Surrender only considers the concept of giving and need alone.

Surrender is not one giant thing that we do one time and then it becomes a way of life. There are thousands of tiny surrenders every day. That is the only way that pride is whipped. Pride is a part of human nature. I want to tap into that divine nature that is in me. One time, I was sitting in class at a school of biblical studies, and of course, we were tested on the instruction we received. Some answers on the test were very objective, and they were either right or wrong, of course. Some answers that called on us to evaluate and answer subjectively were determined by our understanding. The purpose was to decide whether we had an adequate grasp of the subject. Sometimes the answers were close, but what we concluded did not adequately communicate that we understood. One time, we were going over a test, and one of my classmates was more concerned about his grade than his understanding. He questioned the instructor about an answer, as to whether or not it was right. He made his argument to the instructor in front of the entire class. It had elements of truth, but the overall answer was incorrect. He persisted with the teacher for a correct answer. The teacher, being a godly, humble man, wanted to help but, to be true to the rest of the class, simply said, "It is not altogether right. So if you will, let this be a test of your surrender." That is what it is about. It is a test of surrender in my life. It is not one giant surrender that happens when I become a follower of Jesus. It is little bits of surrender that happen every day in many ways. It comes in many forms. But it is always a test of my surrender. That is the way pride is overcome. Always remember, "Inch by inch it is a cinch. Yard by yard it is too hard." So look for the tests of surrender, especially when it comes to the cheek, the cloak, and the kilometer.

SIXTEEN

Love Your Enemies—
Attitude toward Maturity

You have heard that it was said, "Love your
neighbor and hate your enemy." But I tell you,
Love your enemies and pray for those who
persecute you, that you may be sons of your Father
in heaven. He causes His sun to rise on the evil
and the good, and sends rain on the righteous and
the unrighteous. If you love those who love you,
what reward will you get? Are not even the tax
collectors doing that? And if you greet only your
brothers, what are you doing more than others? Do
not even the pagans do that? Be perfect, therefore,
as your heavenly Father is perfect.
—MATTHEW 5:43–48

suppose of all the things that Jesus taught, this one gives me more trouble than most. A few years back, I knew a man that was elected the business representative of a local painters' union. There were several folks running for that position. He did not get the majority of votes in the union. He simply got a majority of votes to win because of so many people trying to get the position. Because he only got enough votes to win, he found himself being opposed by the ones who ran against him as well as those who voted for them. He was in a position of being opposed on several different sides. This was a problem for him. He tried to reason with them. He tried to be cordial. He tried to work for the good of everyone. He found himself being tugged by the evil one to retaliate. He found himself being coerced to get back at them for what they were doing to him. That translated to the membership as a whole. He was confused. This was directly opposed to what he stood for. They knew that too. They pushed it to the limits. This lasted for about six months. So he started doing something that they did not know about. He started praying for them one by one. He called their names before God. He simply did what Jesus said. Then one by one, a change began to take place. Do not misunderstand—not everyone changed. But most did and the remainder of his term went rather well, and several things were accomplished for the common good. But some of those who opposed him became some of his best allies and friends.

The concept of loving and praying for enemies is not something that is easy. It is often difficult. But this concept is a little bigger than I am able to wrap my mind around. When Jesus spoke these words on the mount, He opened the door for understanding something about the nature of God. It was something that was higher, nobler, and more mature than His Jewish children were practicing in their lives. It is also true of me. Loving and praying for my enemies goes beyond "normal" maturity levels. It is obvious this is true because if they already practiced it, He would not have had to speak about it. Loving my enemies goes directly against what I want to do. So in order to understand this, Jesus appealed to the maturity level of God Almighty to illustrate it for me.

He continues with His comparisons. He compares loving my neighbor and hating my enemies to loving my enemies. The attitude behind this command is found in an attitude toward maturity. It is the attitude of God. It is the attitude of God toward me when Jesus went to the cross. I was opposed to Him. I was the enemy because of sin. Yet in His maturity, He loved me to the point that He died for me. This is God's maturity. It is higher than my ways. Yet it is this way that I am called.

Actually, we are talking about relationships with others. Immature relationships are relationships that only love those who love me. It is decided by the response received. Immature relationships hate those who oppose me. In reality, it is not the relationship that is immature. It is the one who is engaged in the relationship. It goes to the maturity level of the person, not the relationship.

On the flip side, maturity loves those who oppose me. Maturity prays for people who persecute me. You see, that is a family trait. It comes from the Father. That is the way He is. It is not because of me and who I am. It is because of my relationship with the Father that this can be carried out. He is the one who gets the glory for this type of maturity.

Jesus describes the maturity of the Father in this way: He causes the sun to rise on the just and the unjust. He sends the rain on the righteous and the unrighteous. God's maturity does not differentiate blessings based on those who follow Him and those who do not. This is a big deal. The immaturity of His followers makes this a big deal. This is why His followers tend to ask the question "Why?" when the unrighteous are blessed. This is the reason that Christians wonder when ungodly people prosper. This is the reason that I am in conflict when unscrupulous folks have excellent health. It goes back to maturity levels. I want the Father to bring the hammer down on the bad hearts and bless the good ones. I want health to be broadcast to Christians who follow God and limited to those who do not. God's maturity does not do that. He blesses both. He responds to both in love regardless of their response. That is maturity.

Jesus describes the immaturity of man in this way: Immaturity will love only those who love them. The question is, how is this any different? How is this a level that is higher and nobler? Well, it is not. That is where Jesus raises the bar, again. He says that even dishonest people are capable of that level of maturity. His illustration to the Jews is that even tax collectors love those who love them. The Jews knew who the tax collectors were. They were the dishonest people who cheated, extorted, and stole money. Even these people loved those who loved them. It took no maturity to do that.

Immaturity will also greet only brothers. This is not a higher calling. It is the same thing that pagans do. They greet their brothers. It is easy to greet those who greet you. People with no maturity do that. The pagans were considered uncivilized by the Jews. They held them in contempt. Yet Jesus compared this level of maturity to theirs. The question becomes then, why is this immature?

This is immature because greeting only my brothers and loving only those who love me is predicated on their response. I love and greet because I know they will love me back and greet me as well. It takes no maturity to do that. When those who love me turn on me, what will be my response then? When brothers get a burr under their saddle and do not greet me, what will be my response then? They become folks who oppose me or even become my enemies. How will I respond then? It will take a higher level of maturity on my part.

Jesus is trying to help me understand that maturity responds consistently with love regardless of the response of others. This is the way God responds. His maturity responds with love for those who love Him. His maturity responds with love for those who oppose Him. He is mature. So be mature like the Father. This is what His children do. It is a family trait that comes from His nature. This really raises the bar. It takes relationships to a new level. It allows this disciple to transcend the pride and selfishness of my human nature. It allows me to become a partaker of His divine nature. Only God's nature shows maturity on this level. This type of maturity is only existent because of God. He showed us. He lived it for us. He continues to show us every day. Each morning when the sun peeks up over these West Virginia hills, God shows His maturity. Every time the rain clouds gather, God's maturity is being presented to me as a show-and-tell of His maturity. So Jesus calls us to be mature as the Father is mature.

There are many lessons that this maturity teaches. It teaches me that love and prayer for my enemies transcends immaturity. This is a way to divine maturity. Maturity is what we, as disciples, are longing for. That is one way that we can follow in the steps of the Mature One. Make it a point to pray for those who oppose you. This brings God's hand into the equation. He can do things and change people that you and I could never dream of doing or changing. He may intervene. He may not. The key is that I am of an attitude to pray for them and their best interest.

This level of maturity also allows for the release of bitterness. Bitterness stems from my nature. Maturity comes from God's nature because He is maturity. When His nature becomes my nature, then bitterness is released. It is pretty difficult to pray to the God of the universe through clenched teeth.

Another aspect of this maturity is that through love and prayer, foes can become friends. God is amazing in His work. He can change lives. He is still working on me. But if He can change this man who used to be His enemy, He can change the fellow who is my enemy too. This is the point. Maturity helps us to understand just how precious God's creation is to Him. People are precious to God. He wants them to be precious to me too. This level of maturity is how they become precious to me. When this happens, then He is glorified not only by my maturity but also by the result of love and prayer for others. He is glorified when I consistently treat others based on His maturity. He is glorified when those foes become friends through love and prayer. He is glorified even if they do not become friends, by a consistent life of maturity.

Maturity also reminds me that I do not serve God in order to be blessed but because I already am blessed. I do not respond to opposition in order to be blessed by God. I do not fulfill this directive by the Lord in order to receive a blessing. I fulfill this directive because the mature Father of the universe has already blessed me.

The conclusion of the matter is from the mouth of Jesus. His conclusion is drawn by His "therefore" in the last line. Therefore, Jesus says, be mature like your heavenly Father is mature. Lord, help me to be mature.

IN BETWEEN

Well, we have finished Matthew Chapter 5. It has been a pretty quick trip, so let's hit the Pause button for a minute and let it digest for a while. There have been some pretty deep things that we have talked about. Some are pretty difficult. They are for me anyway. The purpose of these things is not to be heavy but to lighten. When I take the principles of the beatitudes and apply them to these things, then they become lighter. The heart changes first, then the actions follow. This lightens the load. Purpose, motivation, relationships, temptation, faithfulness, truthfulness, surrender, and maturity all take on new meanings when I view them in light of the maturity of the disciple found in the beatitudes. That is why the beatitudes are the essence of the essence. Did you check out how the beatitudes were involved in these sections? Did you see how some could go through the whole list?

If my concern is pleasing God, then these things can and will be life-changing. It can move me to a deeper understanding of God and what He wants in my life. It can give a relief that no one else could ever give. It takes away all the pretenses. I do not have to live up to others' expectations. It only requires beginning with humility, and everything else will fall into place. That is where it becomes freeing. It is through these that the rest of Matthew Chapter 5 comes alive. I hope you have enjoyed the trip so far. The rest of the trip *is* just as enjoyable. OK, you can hit the Pause button again, and we will keep going. God bless.

SEVENTEEN

Acts of Righteousness Part 1– Attitude toward Serving

Be careful not to do your "acts of righteousness" before men, to be seen by them. If you do, you will have no reward from your Father in heaven. So, when you give to the needy, do not announce it with trumpets, as the hypocrites do in the synagogues and on the streets, to be honored by men. I tell you the truth, they have received their reward in full. But when you give to the needy, do not let your left hand know what your right hand is doing, so that your giving may be in secret. Then your Father, who sees what is done in secret, will reward you.

–Matthew 6:1–4

Have you ever driven home from work and when you got home, you did not remember a thing about the trip? I mean, did you not remember passing different things on the way? Maybe it happens because you were thinking about something. Maybe it is because you were listening to the radio. Maybe it happens because it is a routine thing. Sometimes the routine can occur without too much thought about it. You know it can happen in our service and worship to God as well. Ever been to church and, when it is over, you cannot recall what the sermon was about? When everything is said and done, you cannot remember what songs were sung or what the prayers were. I find myself in this position at times. Maybe it is because my worship is routine. Maybe it is because the purpose of my worship has been lost.

I believe that the Jews found themselves in this position. The things they did to worship God were right. It was right to do acts of righteousness. It was right to give to the needy. It was right to do good things. It is important to do the right things. God wants worship to be right. Look at Nadab and Abihu (Leviticus 10:1–2). There was a prescribed plan laid out for worship. They changed it and were fried like two pieces of bacon. God is interested in doing things right. But unfortunately, Jesus said on the mount that the Jews were doing the right things wrong. Their motive for doing the right things was wrong. Now, things are changing. Not only does God want the right things, but God wants the right things done right. He is interested in the motive as well as the action.

The next three sections deal with the right things: giving to the needy, prayer, and fasting. All three are right things, yet Jesus condemned the way they were doing the right things. In this section, we will deal with giving to the needy. Jesus compares two things: announcing my giving to the needy versus giving to the needy in secret. What Jesus is trying to change is the attitude toward righteousness. That is the underlying principle behind these directives. The purpose behind what I do becomes especially important.

The purpose of the Jews giving to the needy was to bring recognition for themselves. They would blow trumpets both in church and on the street so that other people would recognize their good deeds. This may be where the term "blowing your own horn" comes from. Their purpose was not so much to give to the needy but to be seen giving to the needy, to be recognized for it. Jesus compared them to hypocrites. Hypocrites wear two different outfits. They wear two different masks. One outfit is solely for themselves. The other is for others to see. They act in two different ways. One way is the reality of how they are. The other way is the perception, how they want others to think of them. This goes to the heart of righteousness. Righteousness is never perception. It has no bearing based on others' perceptions. Perception is merely from the teeth out. Perception considers only the look of righteousness. What is in the heart is of no consequence when perception is involved.

Jesus is trying to change the mindset about what righteousness really is. The attitude of righteousness does not involve men's perceptions of me. It involves only God's knowing who I am. God is the only one that counts. You see, I can be fooled. Anyone can pull the wool over my eyes. I am a pretty trusting sort. Just about anyone can make me think they are exceptional in their service. That is OK. But I am not the one who makes the determination about the heart. God cannot be fooled. God cannot be mocked (Galatians 6:7). He knows the heart. All the glitz and glimmer does not dress a heart. It is completely open before God (John 2:25). That is why Jesus is trying to change the attitude toward righteousness.

Jesus says to do the acts of righteousness in secret. Do not let anyone see what you do. He changes everything that the Jews thought religion and righteousness were. This righteousness is different because God is involved in it. My giving to the needy is not for the purpose of building me up. It is for the purpose of glorifying God. If glory to God is my motive for serving, then no one has to see me do it.

Even if I am doing the right thing, if I do it with no thought of God, it becomes a selfish misnomer. God is interested in doing the right thing right. Doing it right involves God as the motive for doing it. It involves God's glory as the underlying motive. Yes, the needy are helped, and that is wholly valid. But helping the needy for my ego or my honor translates to using their needs for my benefit. When I do that, then my only reward is the honor that I receive from men for what I have done. That reward is fleeting. It is temporary. It lacks substance because it is only perception.

If my motive for helping the needy is to glorify God, then the needy are helped and God is glorified. It does not matter who is watching or not watching. It is ultimately a relationship between God and me. He is the one that I am trying to please. He is the one who gets the glory. Oh yes, the needy are still helped, but the greater thing is that God is glorified. He is the ultimate rewarder. When I do something to be seen by men, I receive a reward, but my reward is simply what they think about me. When I serve in secret, then no one else knows. When it is so concealed that only God knows, He rewards. He is really good at it too. No one rewards like God. I do not know what the reward is. It may be that the reward is heaven. It may be that it is a spiritual blessing. It may be that it is the pressed down, shaken together, "running over shall He heap into your bosom" type of reward (Luke 6:38). It really does not matter when our motive is the glory of God. That may be the reward too. The conscious understanding that I am trying to glorify God and not myself may be the reward. That is priceless for the disciple. It takes no thought of self. I am *not* the concern. What I get out of all of this does not matter then. God is the central focus of my acts of righteousness.

Now, here are some observations about this matter. Sometimes in order to know what something is, I first have to decide what it is not. It is a definition of the opposite. Righteousness is not a matter of reputation. It does not matter the least bit what men think I am. That has no bearing on what I really am. When I am more concerned with "perception is everything," I lose sight of what is really important. Righteousness is not a matter of what others think I am. I can be a dog-drunk, wife-beating, child-molesting bigot at home and give the perception that I am in the who's who of the top ten Christians in my church. Perception is deceitful. It is a heart problem. Righteousness is not a matter of receiving applause. It does not deal with who knows what I have done. That is not the purpose of righteousness.

Righteousness is a matter of character. That is why when it is done in secret, no one else knows character is matured. Character comes to light even on the darkest night. Character does what is right when no one else is looking. Righteousness is a matter of what God knows. It goes to the core of my relationship with Him. It wants to please Him without thinking of myself. It is also a matter of God's reward. He is good! Imagine Andy Griffith saying it: "He's gooooood." He rewards. Just knowing that God is the rewarder should be enough, huh? That is right. The attitude of righteousness developed in the disciple who does the right things right, and is rewarded by the God of the universe, is the place that I have come to.

So my worship and my service when elevated to God's plane and for His glory will not become something that He did not intend. There will be a change for the believer. It will free me up. No longer do I have to make sure the leaders notice. I will not have to have my name in the bulletin. I will not have to have a plaque on the wall. The fellowship hall will not have to be named after me. I can worship and serve and know all the time where I have passed. I will remember the sermon, the songs, and the prayers because the focus is on God. It will not be a routine thing. It will be a righteous thing before God to His glory. Amen and amen.

EIGHTEEN

Acts of Righteousness Part 2– Attitude toward Prayer

And when you pray, do not be like the hypocrites, for they love to pray standing in the synagogues and on the street corners to be seen by men. I tell you the truth, they have received their reward in full. But when you pray, go into your room, close the door and pray to your Father, who is unseen. Then your Father, who sees what is done in secret, will reward you. And when you pray, do not keep on babbling like pagans, for they think they will be heard because of their many words. Do not be like them, for your Father knows what you need before you ask him. This, then is how you should pray: "Our Father in heaven, hallowed be your name, your kingdom come, your will be done on earth as it is in heaven. Give us today our daily bread. Forgive us our debts, as we also have forgiven our debtors. And lead us not into temptation but deliver us from the evil one for yours is the kingdom and the power and the glory forever, Amen." For if you forgive men when they sin against you, your heavenly Father will also forgive you. But if you do not forgive men their sins, your Father will not forgive your sins.
–MATTHEW 6:5–15

C ommunication is vital. It is vital in every relationship. The importance of communicating with people cannot be overemphasized. It is the eyes, the facial expressions, the hand gestures, the tone of my voice, the inflection of my words— all a part of communicating with people. Each of these elements reflects the heart as much as the words I am speaking. When I talk with people, these things are vital in helping to communicate. The reason these are vital is that people cannot look into the heart. They can only hear and see the outward expression. There is a major difference in my communication with God. God does not need these things when I speak with Him. He can see my heart. He knows my motives. He knows my feelings. He knows my logic. He simply knows my heart. This is prayer. Prayer is my communication to God.

Communication is vital. It is a vital part of this relationship with the Lord. That is why Jesus chose to explain this act of righteousness in such a descriptive way. That is why he chose to explain this communication so we could understand its importance. He knew the Jewish concept of prayer. He knew what they had seen. He heard their performances. He knew to whom they were praying. So He chose to teach them about communicating to God.

Jesus again draws a comparison. The comparison is between praying to be seen by men and praying to be seen by God. There were many Jews who thought communication with God was a status. They were caught up in the perception of men again. They thought that their prayers were indicative to others of their holiness. They loved this. It was not that they loved the communication with God, but they loved the perception it brought concerning them. They flaunted their prayers. They would pray in the synagogues and on the street corners. Jesus exposed their motives. It was not that it was wrong to pray. It was not wrong at all. It became wrong because of the reason they prayed in the synagogues and street corners. Their motives were to receive glory from men. They were not praying to be heard by God but rather to be heard by men. Their motives were to portray that they were close to God when in fact they were hypocrites.

Their prayers were long and flowery. They prayed and prayed and prayed. They equated long prayers with God's hearing. If they prayed long enough and babbled like the pagans, then they would be heard. Jesus said that their reward was already received. Their reward was the fact that men heard and oohed and aahed. It was for their individual glory from men.

Jesus wants His disciples to pray differently. He wants prayer to be between God and them alone. So in order to accomplish this purpose, He wants them to go into a private solitary place and talk to God. It is at that point that all barriers are broken down. When I am by myself praying to the Father, there can be no man to impress with my prayer. It is then that prayer is placed on the heart level and not the perception level. It is there that God is glorified.

After Jesus explains how not to pray, He starts instructing how to pray. One line of the instruction says that the Father knows what you need before you ask. If the Father knows what I need before I ask, why do I need to pray? That is a perplexing question. Why can't He just go ahead and fulfill my needs? I believe the reason is that we will know when He does answer our prayers and we will know that He is the one who did it. If God arbitrarily filled my cup with blessings, I may tend to attribute it to coincidence or think I was responsible for the blessings. One reason I pray is so that when the prayer is answered, I know He is the one who did it. It gives Him the glory and not me.

Here is how we ought to pray. This is what the Son of God says about communicating with the Father. I believe that it reflects ten things that we can include in our prayers. Jesus knew how to communicate with the Father. I do not know how Jesus could be more specific than saying to His disciples, "This is how you should pray."

How to pray:

1. *To the Father—Our Father in heaven.* The Father is the one to whom I should pray. It is not to someone else. My prayer is to the Father because He is the one who hears and answers. Then He is the one who receives the glory.
2. *Praise/Glory—Hallowed be Your name.* My prayer should start with praise and glory to the Holy One. He is the one to be glorified. His disciples need to be proactive in giving Him glory. We should not be passive and assume that He is being glorified. It is my calling as a disciple to glorify the Father intentionally and on purpose. That is why we are here.
3. *Evangelism—Your kingdom come.* Some believe that this is archaic because the kingdom of God already came. Well, I believe it is a valid thing. People are either in the kingdom of God or the kingdom of darkness. When folks are translated into the kingdom of God from the kingdom of darkness (Colossians 1:13), then the kingdom or the rule of God has come into their lives. Jim McGuiggan has a good discussion of this idea of the kingdom of God in his book *The Reign of God.*[15] It is worth reading. When people surrender to Him, He then becomes their king. This is a prayer for the salvation of humankind. It is an integral concept of the Lord and His disciples.
4. *Purpose—Your will be done.* The will of the Father is all-important. It stands opposed to my will. Faith is the idea of making the Father's will my will. It is the purpose of the

---

[15]   Jim McGuiggan, *The Reign of God,* (Lubbock, Texas: Montex Publishing Company, 1979) p. 67

universe. Everything was created according to His will. It is why this little planet still exists. It is based on His will. That is our purpose, to conform to His will.

5. *Providence—Give us this day our daily bread.* This is a plea for God's providing for the necessities of life. Those are things that I take for granted. I assume that I will eat. I am called upon to be dependent upon God for His providence in my life. So I entreat the Father to provide these necessities.

6. *Forgiveness—Forgive us our debts.* This is the prayer for just what we need. It also implies that we need forgiveness for something. It is the contrite confession of a sinner who is in desperate need of God's amazing grace. It is the only thing that can set the stage for what follows.

7. *Mercy—As we forgive our debtors.* Comparative forgiveness is what we are asking for. God forgives **as** we forgive. If I do not forgive totally but reserve the right to hold back and carry around baggage, then forgiveness is presented to me in the same way. This is a prayer to help me to forgive like God does. This is a prayer for my showing mercy as I have received it.

8. *Guidance—Lead us not into temptation.* This part of the prayer reflects my need for His leadership in my life. The prayer is that His paths do not lead me to places where temptation comes. It precedes the next element of prayer.

9. *Protection—Deliver us from the evil one.* This is the element that is difficult for me to understand. I do not rightly know the immense power of the evil one. Jesus did. He knows that I am no match for the evil one by myself. I need the protection of the Father. He is the omnipotent one. He is the one who can thwart the power of the evil one, and I need His protection in the matter.

10. *Praise/Glory—Yours is the kingdom and the power and the glory forever. Amen.* Prayer is to end just like it is started. The glory of the Father is first and last. It is the beginning and end of every communication with Him. It is to this end that I should spend my time and pray my prayers.

So using these ten things is how Jesus taught His disciples to pray. I would do well to incorporate these concepts into my prayer life as well. It is one thing to be instructed on how not to pray. It is a completely different ball game when the Lord says this is how you should pray. That is pretty plain. It is also pretty helpful in this communication process called prayer.

This section also has some unique observations about the relationship I have with God through prayer. Prayer is not to preach a sermon to the church or to others. Its purpose is to talk with God. It is between God and me. It is great to love to pray. Jesus wants us to love to pray. He also wants me to love to pray for the right reason. That is an integral ingredient in this act of righteousness.

Prayer for the purpose of being seen and heard by men has no merit. Prayer in secret has great merit. One prayer tends to glorify me by what and how I say it. The other prayer glorifies God by the one who hears it. Prayer is to be God-centered. He is the focus, not me.

The perpendicular relationship I have with God is dependent upon my parallel relationships with others. Forgiveness is based on forgiveness. Mercy is based on mercy. This is a big deal. It is like the section "Anger and the Altar." Both worship and forgiveness are dependent upon our treatment of others. It is a call to comparative forgiveness. God will forgive *as* we forgive. That puts forgiveness into a completely different perspective.

Here is a story from the mission field. There are many stories about prayer, but this one is especially touching to me.

Charlie McKinney and his family spent a few years in Brazil as missionaries. One time, he and one of his coworkers, Ron Bontrager, knew that a Christian and his family had fallen on extremely hard times. So they went to the grocery store and loaded up with food and necessities to take to the family. They carried the sacks of groceries up to the door and knocked. The brother answered the door, and the whole family was with him. They all began to cry. Charlie and Ron were touched by their gratitude. They found out later that the reason they were crying was because the family had been in prayer. They had nothing to eat in the house and no money to buy anything. They had gathered to pray that God would "give them this day their daily bread." When the Christian said, "Amen" at the end of His prayer, Charlie and Ron knocked at the door. Their tears were tears of thanksgiving to the Father, who supplied their need, and they knew it. Jesus said, "This, then, is how you should pray."

NINETEEN

Acts of Righteousness Part 3– Attitude toward Fasting

When you fast, do not look somber as the hypocrites do, for they disfigure their faces to show men they are fasting. I tell you the truth, they have received their reward in full. But when you fast, put oil on your head and wash your face, so that it will not be obvious to men that you are fasting, but only to your Father, who is unseen; and your Father, who sees what is done in secret, will reward you.
–MATTHEW 6:16–18

Whenever I take a good thing and change it into something that was not intended, its purpose is changed. When the purpose is changed, then the good thing is changed into something not-so-good. The purpose of the temple was to worship. There were some in Jesus's time that changed that purpose into a moneymaking scheme. They sold birds and animals for sacrifice. They exchanged money from one currency to another. This made God angry, and He made a whip and drove them out of the temple (John 2:12–16). The Lord seems to be serious about His purposes. I understand that this may be on a different plane from exchanging worship for another purpose, but in theory, it is the same. Changing something from its good, intended purpose to something else makes a big difference.

The same is true with good deeds or prayer or fasting. These things that Jesus talked about on the mount were things that the Jews were remarkably familiar with. They were not an exhaustive list of acts of righteousness, but these three were righteous acts. There is a big difference between just going through the motions of some righteousness and having a heart for righteousness. The prime example is God Himself. Would it not be disheartening if God just did the things He does and He really did not want to do them? Would it not change my response to Him? Wouldn't it be hurtful if I thought that He really did not want to forgive my sins, but He did it anyway because that was what was expected of Him? It changes everything.

The same is true of my motives toward righteousness. It is true toward good deeds. It is true of prayer. This is also true of fasting. The Master, in His comparisons of fasting, uses the same logic. Jesus is still trying to change the heart. He compares fasting that is seen by men with fasting seen by God. These, of course, are two completely different motives. Fasting for the purpose of being seen by men carries with it the idea of personal glory. Fasting for the purpose of being seen by God carries with it the idea of God's glory. The first example is what Jesus calls hypocritical fasting. Men disfigured their faces. They looked somber. They tried to show that fasting really took a toll on them. They wanted others to know that they were fasting. They thought it made them look holy and close to God. Jesus says when folks see that type of fasting, it is their only reward.

The fast that Jesus speaks about is different. It is a fast that stems from the heart. It is personal and uses discretion. It is not something that calls attention to the one who fasts. Jesus wants fasting to be done in a way that is not obvious to others. It is not for the purpose of drawing attention. It is not a matter of being somber, changing the countenance, and disfiguring the face. It is a matter of being spic 'n span. It is a matter of being joyful. It is a matter of not even giving the appearance to others that the fast is taking place. When that type of fasting occurs, then the Father is glorified in my life, and He is the one who rewards.

Jesus was speaking to Jews. Remember, these were the covenant children of God. Now, we who are Christians are the covenant children of God. When Jesus spoke, He used specific terminology. He did not say *if* you fast. He said *when* you fast. "*If* I fast" relates to the possibility that I may not fast. It carries with it the idea that it is optional. On the other side, "*when* I fast" implies the idea that it is going to happen. The question is not that it may happen. The assumption is when it happens. *When* implies that it is not an optional thing. It implies that it is going to occur, but there is a time when it does. This is an important issue. *When* takes it out of the element of being optional for the covenant child. It puts it into the realm of necessity or command. So why does Jesus treat fasting with so much emphasis? There are certain things that are related to fasting that the disciple needs as a part of his life.

Fasting is a personal relationship. It creates a dependence

upon God during the time of the fast. It makes me rely on God for the strength to get through it. It makes me depend on Him when I am weak. It is part of the discipline idea. Discipline brings with it control. Control is something that every disciple needs in order to control the urges the tempter places in front of us. Meekness is the response of the soul that mourns. I need that control. The idea of fasting creates reliance upon God for that control or meekness. He is the one who gives the strength to carry it through. It also reminds me of God's presence in my life. When my old belly growls, I am reminded of God and my need for Him. That is an adequate reminder of God in my life.

Fasting is also connected to humility. In Ezra 8:21–23, Ezra called for a fast "so that we might humble ourselves before God." Fasting is related to humility or being poor in spirit. That is the bottom line of it all. Humility is the key that unlocks the door to God's grace because "God opposes the proud but gives grace to the humble" (James 4:6). Anything that will help in developing humility becomes a grace thing. If fasting helps me to develop humility, then I welcome it.

Fasting is related to repentance as well. In Jonah 3:6–10, the story of Nineveh's repentance is told. "When the news reached the king of Nineveh, he rose from his throne, took off his royal robes, covered himself with sackcloth, and sat down in the dust. Then he issued a proclamation in Nineveh: 'By the decree of the king and his nobles: Do not let any man or beast, herd or flock, taste anything; do not let them eat or drink. But let man and beast be covered with sackcloth. Let everyone call urgently on God. Let them give up their evil ways and their violence. Who knows? God may yet relent and with compassion turn from His fierce anger so that we will not perish.' Then God saw what they did and how they turned from their evil ways, He had compassion and did not bring upon them the destruction He had threatened." It sounds like fasting is related to many things in the beatitudes. It involves both humility and repentance. These are echoes of the poor in spirit and of mourning. But there is another purpose behind fasting.

The church in Acts 13:2–3 fasted and prayed for two different reasons. One was for what I believe to be sanctification. Sanctification is one of those two-dollar words that seem to slip by me. It simply means to be made holy or suitable for God's service. That is what the church was praying for. These men were set apart for God's work. They were also set apart for evangelism. They became missionaries. They went out from among them to preach to others about Jesus. Fasting was related to the initiation of both.

Fasting has an important place in the life of a disciple. It has unfortunately been my experience that fasting has not been seen with the emphasis that Jesus placed upon it on the mount. It can lead to humility, repentance, and sanctification. All are elements of the heart that the believer in Jesus wants as a part of their lives. Jesus knows that fasting is one way that these can be initiated. He calls on His people to fast.

He does not say if. He says when. So maybe fasting can become more of a part of my life. Maybe it can help my attitude toward poor in spirit, mourning, meekness, and the hungering and thirsting after righteousness. Lord, give me the strength and the will to fast.

TWENTY

True Treasures—
Attitude toward Affection/Loyalty

Do not store up for yourselves treasures on earth,
where moth and rust destroy, and where thieves
break in and steal. But store up for yourselves
treasures in heaven, where moth and rust do not
destroy, and where thieves do not break in and
steal. For where your treasure is, there your heart
will be also. The eye is the lamp of the body. If
your eyes are good, your whole body will be full of
light. But if your eyes are bad, your whole body will
be full of darkness. If then the light within you is
darkness, how great is that darkness! No one can
serve two masters. Either he will hate the one and
love the other, or he will be devoted to the one and
despise the other. You cannot serve both God and
money.
–MATTHEW 6:19–24

t has been said that the devil cannot harm a Christian if he shoots his flaming arrows in the head because he wears the helmet of salvation. He cannot kill him if he shoots him in the chest because he wears the breastplate of righteousness. There is no way to trip him up because he is wearing the shoes of the preparation of the gospel. Other fiery darts are quenched with the shield of faith. But the devil can slip around behind one and shoot him in the billfold and kill him almost every time.

This is one section where Jesus goes to the heart of the issue, whether it is on a hill in the first century or on one in the twenty-first century. It deals with treasures. It deals with the will of man. It deals with the affections of man. It deals with the loyalty of man. Jesus is talking to Jews who took a great deal of interest in treasures. It was common then. It is common now. A preacher can talk for months about things to change in my life. He can preach about prayer, fasting, and doing good deeds. He can preach about changing the heart. These things can affect me, and I will listen to this teaching with ease. But talk about money, and ears perk up all over the place. That is something really close to the heart.

When Jesus talked about treasures on the mount, I am sure their ears perked up too. Jesus makes another comparison. It is about treasure. It deals with the physical versus the spiritual. Jesus compares treasures on earth with treasures in heaven. Treasures on earth have some common elements. They will not last because they will decay. They are susceptible to theft because thieves will break through and steal them. There is always the worry about losing them or their losing value. The true treasures on the other hand are treasures in heaven. They are spiritual treasures. Neither decay nor thieves have any bearing on them. These treasures are the only treasures that will last. They are indicative of trust in God. The first indicates trust in self.

The real issue is not the treasure but the heart. Jesus says that treasures and the heart are interrelated. He says that where your treasure is located is where the heart is as well. What does He mean by this? Does He mean that the heart is there because the treasure is there? Or does Jesus mean that the treasure is there because the heart is there?

I believe the latter is true. The heart determines loyalty and allegiance. It determines the value I place on certain things. The heart not only determines what is considered to be a treasure but also places value on it. Whatever I consider to be of value is a treasure to me. If my heart determines that physical treasures are valuable, then that is where my loyalty and affection will be located. I will do whatever it takes to maintain those treasures. If my heart determines that spiritual treasures are valuable, then that is where my loyalty and affection will be located. I will do whatever it takes to maintain those treasures as well.

These two ideas cannot coexist. It is an either/or situation. It is either one or the other. Jesus uses two illustrations to describe this concept. He uses the eye as the lamp of the body and uses the idea of serving two masters.

There is either light or darkness. They cannot coexist. If there is darkness, then there is no light. If there is light, then there is no darkness. If the eye is good, then the whole body is full of light. This is compared to true treasures. It indicates a loyalty and a heart for God. It chooses to do God's bidding and follow His will. If the eye is bad, then the body will be full of darkness. This illustrates the idea of a heart that is not centered on God but wants to do what it wants instead. It is interested in physical treasures instead of spiritual treasures. Here is the problem. If the light, which is supposed to be good, is darkness, there is no light whatsoever. The darkness is too great; everything is darkness. Jesus is saying that light and darkness both cannot coexist. If there is no light, then everything is darkness. There is no light or good involved.

He goes on to describe the relationship of a servant to two masters. No one can loyally serve two masters. This is an either/or situation. Either the servant will serve one master loyally and not serve the second, or he will serve the second loyally and not serve the first. This is the real comparison.

Treasures are indicative of the heart. The heart can only be loyal to one master. The treasures of a person show the loyalty of the heart. If the treasure is physical, then the heart holds loyalty to that treasure. If the treasure is spiritual, then loyalty is to that treasure. There is no room for divided loyalty. Jesus says that a man cannot serve both God and money. These two cannot coexist. The loyalties and affections of a disciple are either toward God or toward money. The divided loyalty of the heart cannot coexist any more than light can coexist with darkness.

The whole section deals with who has my trust. If God has my trust, then my treasures will be laid up in heaven. If my trust is in physical wealth, then my treasures are stored on earth. The treasure, whatever it is, is determined by what the heart considers to be of value. When I consider something to be of value, then it has my loyalty and affection. If it has my loyalty and affection, then that is what my heart considers worth serving. The treasure is an indicator of the loyalty, affection, and service of the heart. There cannot be two treasures any more than I can have light and darkness. There cannot be two treasures any more than I can serve two masters. The treasure is indicative of where my trust is located.

Jesus begins calling for a choice. There is one instrument that God will not play. God will not play second fiddle. He did not create this world to play second fiddle. That is why He told Moses that Israel was to have no other gods before Him (Exodus 20:3). He is the only God. That is what He wants in the lives of His disciples. It is a call to a decision. That is how He made me. He made me to be capable of making a decision. He wants that decision to be for Him. He is the Creator. He is either everything to me or nothing to me. There is no middle ground. This is powerful. For many, this is difficult. How do I respond? Lord, you are my Master.

TWENTY-ONE

First Things First—Attitude toward Trust

Therefore I tell you, do not worry about your life, what you will eat or drink; or about your body, what you will wear. Is not life more important than food, and the body more important than clothes? Look at the birds of the air; they do not sow or reap or store away in barns, and yet your heavenly Father feeds them. Are you not much more valuable than they? Who of you by worrying can add a single hour to his life? And why do you worry about clothes? See how the lilies of the field grow. They do not labor or spin. Yet I tell you that not even Solomon in all his splendor was dressed like one of these. If that is how God clothes the grass of the field, which is here today and tomorrow is thrown into the fire, will He not much more clothe you, O you of little faith? So do not worry, saying, "What shall we eat?" or "What shall we drink?" or "What shall we wear?" For the pagans run after all these things, and your heavenly Father knows that you need them. But seek first His kingdom and His righteousness, and all these things will be given to you as well. Therefore, do not worry about tomorrow, for tomorrow will worry about itself. Each day has enough trouble of its own.
—MATTHEW 6:25–34

n a society that is taken by divided affections, worry is a common thread that unites classes. Folks are always being deceived by Satan to think that things are more important than just about anything else. Worry has become something that traps with jaws more lethal than bear traps. People who have plenty worry about losing what they have. People who have just enough worry about losing what they have or not having enough. It is a cycle that can ensnare, no matter where a person is on the socioeconomic ladder.

I had a friend in school who taught me a valuable lesson about things. He was a young man of about twenty-five. His Father spent his life trying to become a millionaire. He finally accomplished his goal. The young man told me about his family life. He told me about growing up in a home that was obsessed with keeping what they had accumulated. I asked him what his father did when he became a millionaire. He said that his father started working on his second million. His father did not approve of the young man going to a Bible school. His father would not help him in any way. The young man believed it was more important to try to learn about his heavenly Father's ways. So he drove an old Rambler with a shift on the column. He had trouble with the brakes too. Most days, I drove to school. Some days, he drove to school. When we came to the traffic light, he would gear the car down and we would open the doors and try to help stop it with our feet. I asked him why he did not ask his father for help. He said that his father would only help him if he would join him in the family business. He chose the correct family business. He chose to go about his heavenly Father's business. He chose wisely.

He could have had the best food, clothes, cars, and money to burn. He chose something that required trust. This life he chose was not guaranteed to give the best of everything, but it did give the best. He chose to trust God for what he needed. Trust is a big thing in the life of a believer. Jesus knew that when He spoke on the mount as well. He told of the lives of many believers who sought physical things and became anxious about them. He wanted to change their attitude toward trust so they could live lives that brought God glory.

He again used a comparison. The comparison was worry about food and drink versus life, and clothes versus the body. Jesus says not to worry about life in regard to what I will eat or drink. He also says not to worry about the body in regard to what I will wear. Jesus says that life is more important than food and the body is more important than clothes. He then uses two illustrations that drive home the point. The birds of the air do not sow, reap, or store up their food. Yet the heavenly Father feeds them. The lilies of the field do not labor to make clothes. But the heavenly Father clothes them to the point that Solomon in all the splendor of Israel was not clothed like them.

Here is the point. To God, people are more important than anything else. If God takes care of the birds and the flowers, He will take care of me. People are of value to the Lord that is not comparable to things. Compared to birds, we are of much more value. Compared to lilies, we are of much more value. If He takes care of birds and lilies in such a wonderful way, He will take care of you and me even more.

This is where trust comes in. It is a matter of faith. Trusting God eliminates worry. What is the value of worry? What does it do? Who can add an hour to his life by worry? Worry accomplishes nothing. Worry is simply indicative of little faith. It is here that Jesus draws the correlation between worry and little faith. To some, worry is seen as an indicator of caring. If I worry about something, then I care about it. Worry is not an indicator of caring but of a lack of trust. The implication of worry is "I am not in control, but I want to be." The implication of trust is "God is in control." Jesus wants His people to trust God for everything. That is the difference between the faithful and the faithless. This is the contrast. The faithless worry about "What shall I eat?" The faithless worry about "What shall I drink?" The faithless worry about "What shall I wear?" Jesus says that the pagans run after all these things and the Father knows that I need them.

The faithful simply seek first His kingdom and His righteousness. Since the Father knows my needs, all these things will be added to me. That is the contrast. Trusting God's power to provide rather than trusting my power to provide *is* the contrast. That is the key. It goes to the will. Shall I seek my will for my providence, or shall I seek the Father's will for providence? Here is the conflict again. What I want may be more important to me than what God wants in His will.

It is not just the big spiritual wars that go on in my life that are important. It is the basic thing of life. This is where the war of wills starts. It takes *faithful people* willing to trust God *to be faithful people.* Folks who worry are dependent upon themselves. When I cannot supply all the wants of my will, then worry takes over.

The question is, who am I to imitate? Am I to imitate the pagans who want more and more and more, or am I to imitate the faithful who trust in God according to His will? This is the challenge: seek His kingdom and His righteousness, and trust God for everything else while I am seeking.

I believe this is one observation that needs to be made. Previously, Jesus already gave me instructions on how to pray. He said to ask God to "give us this day our daily bread." The section on prayer and the section on serving God versus serving money precede this particular passage for a purpose. That is why Jesus begins this section with "Therefore." The "therefore" is there because of what went before. Those who are concerned with treasures on this earth, eating, drinking, and clothes are folks who are interested in what they want. They worry about all these things. Those who trust in God are focusing on treasures in heaven, life, and the body. The really important thing is living life in the body for the glory of God, seeking His kingdom and His righteousness.

Jesus's conclusion to this matter is very profound. The future is uncertain. So do not worry about tomorrow. Tomorrow will worry for itself. Each day has enough trouble of its own. The present time is all that anyone has. There is no need to borrow trouble. Do not compound living life by worrying about the future. Live one day at a time and trust God.

I know a man who has a degenerative disease. He does not know from day to day what will happen next. He may be blind tomorrow. He may be paralyzed tomorrow. His way of dealing with it is trusting God. He says, "When I wake up in the morning, I wiggle my toes. If they work, I get out of bed." Living one day at a time can only depend on trust in God. This is the attitude toward trust that Jesus is trying to get His disciples to develop. It only comes through the maturity process that begins with humility. Proud people cannot trust God. Lord, give me the faith and humility to trust You.

IN BETWEEN

If I could put Matthew Chapter 6 in a nutshell, it would be this: Jesus wants His disciples to develop a personal relationship with the Father. This personal relationship is based on the heart. It has nothing to do with the way others see me. It is between Him and me alone. It is not for the purpose of others' perceptions. It is for His glory. Whether I help the poor, pray, or fast, Jesus wants me to serve from the heart. It is because of our relationship with the Father that the heart directs our service of righteousness. This personal relationship that nurtures these acts of righteousness comes from an undivided loyalty to Him and an undying trust in Him for everything. Jesus is still building to a climax. Matthew Chapter 6 is in the middle. Now, we move on, and these last attitude changes will call for a decision. See what you think.

TWENTY-TWO

Honest Judgment—
Attitude toward Assessment

Do not judge, or you too will be judged. For in the
same way you judge others, you will be judged,
and with the measure you use, it will be measured
to you. Why do you look at the speck of sawdust
in your brother's eye and pay no attention to the
plank in your own eye? How can you say to your
brother, "Let me take the speck out of your eye,"
when all the time there is a plank in your own eye?
You hypocrite, first take the plank out of your own
eye, and then you will see clearly to remove the
speck from your brother's eye. Do not give dogs
what is sacred; do not throw your pearls to pigs.
If you do, they may trample them under their feet
and then turn and tear you to pieces.
–MATTHEW 7:1–6

J udging is something that seems to come from the dark side. It is something that you would expect Darth Vader to be involved in. In judging, there is always the tendency to look at something or someone else. Usually, judging does not involve me. Judging seems to be something that someone else does toward me and I toward them. This is something that creates problems for people who want to be followers of the Lord. It is a trap that is easily laid. It is also easier to be caught in the trap.

Jesus was very definitive about judging. He told the Jews on the mount, "Do not judge, or you too will be judged." The peril of judging is that it brings the tendency to require more of others than I require of myself. It holds others to a different standard than I am willing to follow. However, the same standard of judgment that I use on others will be applied to me. Whenever I use the standard of God's word as my means of determining what someone else is doing wrong, the standard of God's word is used back toward me. If there is something that my brother is doing wrong and I point it out to him, then he in turn may use the same standard and point out my faults as well.

Jesus implies this type of judging described in this section as dishonest judging. It is implied because of the illustration He uses. This is a very humorous thing. In fact, it is laugh-out-loud funny. The picture is of someone trying to get a small speck of sawdust out of someone's eye while they have a 4" × 4" timber sticking out of their eye. This is an illustration of a man reared as a carpenter. Both the speck of sawdust and the 4" × 4" are wood. The problem is that there is a disproportionate amount of wood in the corrector's eye. Wood compares to sin. It is not the type of sin. It is not that there is a big sin and a little sin. It is the amount of sin. The dishonest judgment lies in my trying to correct my brother's sin when there is a disproportionately greater amount of sin in my own life. The implication is hypocrisy.

What Jesus is trying to do is to get His followers to honestly assess their own lives. Correcting sin is right and just. Removing the speck is good. The point that needs to be made is that it first requires self-assessment. Honesty must be observed in my life to see that there is a plank. Then the plank must be removed from my eye. When I am able to correct my life, then others can be rightly and justly helped to correct their sin. It is dishonest to correct others when I cannot or will not acknowledge my sin and still try to correct theirs.

Does this mean that the preacher has to be perfect before he can preach? Does this mean or imply that I cannot help others with problems in their lives? This is not the emphasis of this section. The emphasis of this section is that I need to actively assess my own life. Of course, this goes back to the "pure in heart" part of the maturing process. The pure heart honestly looks at its own life. The pure heart wants to do what is right. It is constantly making midcourse corrections. That enables the pure heart to help in changing others. This section is trying to change the attitude toward honest self-assessment. Jesus does not intend for His people to be finger-pointing, judgmental, self-righteous, hypocritical people. He wants His people to be folks who want to do what is right. Then His people help others to do what is right. The standard is God's word. The standard will still be there no matter how I live my life. When the preacher preaches, he is not trying to get believers to live up to the standard of his life. He is trying to get folks to look at the standard of God's word. If someone had to be perfect to preach, then only Jesus could preach. The idea is for believers and preachers both to look at God's standard and modify both lives in view of His standard.

Correcting sin is holy. Jesus compares it to a sacred task. He compares it to being as precious as a pearl. This is the point of the dogs and the hogs. When correcting sin becomes dishonest, it holds others to a different standard than I hold myself to. When this hypocrisy occurs, then something as sacred as correcting sin is abused by my life of hypocrisy and double standards. It is like giving what is sacred to the dogs. Double standards and dishonest judging are like throwing pearls to the pigs.

Those dishonest judgments serve no purpose to those who see my hypocrisy. It is like the pigs trampling the pearls. The dishonest judgments that I use toward others then become something that is used against me. That is when the pigs turn on me. The realization of my hypocrisy or my trying to justify myself may then destroy my faith. That is when I am torn to pieces.

Dishonest judgments have a way of destroying me when I do not and am not constantly assessing my own heart. This is what we are called to do. An honest assessment of my own life can lead to the holiness of the correction of sin for me and for others. If I am not honest when I look at my life, then I am not correcting sin in me. If it is not a work in progress in my life, then others will not benefit either. It will hinder their correction too. Some observations that can be made:

1. *Hypocrisy mocks correction.* It puts the holy in the pigpen. It can destroy my faith as well.
2. The return judgment is probably not by God but by the one being judged. *Pride is the culprit.* The one being corrected hits back by being honest with me in my life and points out my faults that I have failed to notice.
3. *One sin is not greater than another sin.* Sin is sin, and both are black as a buzzard's wing. The idea is the amount of sin. Hypocrisy on top of other things makes a 4" x 4".
4. The standard of judgment is essential in convincing or convicting of sin. *God's word is the standard.* It is not my life. It is Jesus's life.

5. Honest judgment comes from honest self-assessment. *It requires honest corrections.* It demands honest concern and love for others. It enables honest correction for both people.

The Master is concerned about the way I view myself more than how I view others. It is a part of the maturing process. It is not intended for disciples to view other disciples in a condescending way. No person is perfect except the Christ. Therefore, as I help and comfort others on their journey, I need to be reminded to be merciful. I need to be reminded about being pure in heart. I need to be reminded to be poor in spirit. The sacred task of correction can only be accomplished when these are present. Honest self-assessment precedes any correction. I must assess myself before any correction is made in my own life. I must assess myself if any correction is attempted in others. If I attempt to help you, it must always start with me. Lord, help me to look honestly at me.

TWENTY-THREE

This Sums It Up—
Attitude toward Selflessness

Ask and it will be given to you; seek and you will
find; knock and the door will be opened to you.
For everyone who asks receives; he who seeks
finds; and to him who knocks, the door will be
opened. Which of you, if his son asks for bread,
will give him a stone? Or if he asks for a fish, will
give him a snake? If you then, though you are evil,
know how to give good gifts to your children, how
much more will your Father in heaven give good
gifts to those who ask him! So, in everything, do
to others what you would have them do to you, for
this sums up the Law and the Prophets.
–MATTHEW 7:7–12

f I were to try to sum up the law and the prophets, I would not sum it up like Jesus does. I would use a word like *burden* or *accusation*. Jesus, who knows what it is all about, does it right. He sums up the law by approaching it the way it was intended rather than what the scribes and Pharisees had made it. Most of the way that I understood the law was from their perspective, not God's. So the same is probably true about the Jews on the mount. Jesus gives a new perspective about the law and one of its real purposes. Yes, the law was intended to expose sin. Yes, the law was to lead the Jews to Jesus and an understanding of grace. But Jesus says in this little section that the thing He is preaching on the mountain sums up the law.

It all reflects the attitude toward selflessness. It goes to the core of the impure heart. It speaks to the part of me that is clogged up with selfishness like glue in the gears. It gives a new, fresh perspective again about what God wants from His disciples' hearts. It is an attitude that will indeed change the way I look at myself and at others.

He begins this section with the idea of asking, seeking, and knocking. There are songs that are written that envelop this thought. Of course, my emphasis of this passage has been to keep on asking, keep on seeking, and keep on knocking. It is something that indicates persistence. Most of the times I have taught or preached this passage, persistence is the thing that I majored in. But I believe, now, that Jesus had something else in mind.

The way that I have looked at this is for my personal gain. If I wanted something, I needed to keep on asking, seeking, and knocking. These things, in my thinking, were all related to me. I would ask to receive it for myself. I would seek to find it for myself. I would knock to have the door opened for me. Jesus then uses an illustration that I would never use in my teaching. I would not relate it to these concepts.

Jesus uses a father/son illustration that drives the point home with me. If a son asks his father for bread, will the father purposefully give him a stone? If a son asks his father for a fish, will the father purposefully give him a snake? The obvious answer is that the father will not give his son an unwanted, unwelcome gift in return for the son's request. Even having a selfish, evil attitude, a father will see to the needs of his son and not be selfish and evil in giving. Even for a father who has a selfish and evil attitude, the father's love of his son will overcome the evil attitude of the father and see to the needs of the son.

Then Jesus makes a comparison between fathers whose attitudes are *evil* and the *how much more* Father in heaven. The Father is beyond compare with this father. His holiness and righteousness are beyond imagination compared to mine. The Father's nature is so much greater than my nature. Now, if I against nature love my son enough to overcome my bad attitudes to give good things to my son, how much more will the Father whose nature is so good and holy be even more willing to give good gifts to His children because of His good and holy nature?

Here is the point of the section. So in everything, implying everybody and everything, I am called upon to treat others selflessly by considering their needs as I would my own needs. Jesus calls upon me to transfer my desire in asking, seeking, and knocking for my own selfishness to others' needs. Treat them as you would like to be treated. I am called upon to keep on asking for them and their need as I would for myself. I am called upon to seek for them as I would for myself. I am encouraged to knock for them as I would myself.

The key is not to try to heap the goodness and generosity of the Father's giving upon me but rather heap the generosity of the Father's giving on others by asking, seeking, and knocking for them. Selflessness and love are the goals of the law and the prophets. This sums it all up. That is why Jesus did not come to destroy the law and the prophets. He came to fulfill it. He came to be selfless and to love. He came to do the Father's will, not His. This is the goal of the commands given to regulate relationships. Treat others as you want them to treat you.

Of course, there are other lessons to be found in this passage. There is a need for persistence in our prayer life. It is not a one-shot deal. It is a persistent, ongoing plea for God to intervene. That is a key to prayer, no matter whether it is for me or the ones for whom I pray.

I am by nature selfish. It is a pride thing. Selflessness goes against this nature. Selflessness is a God thing. It only comes from Him and through Him. It is a part of His nature that is in conflict with my nature. Yet even for a father whose nature is proud, that bit of God's nature that is attached through the thread of His nature from creation allows me to show unselfishness to those I love.

The awesomeness of God's goodness is all over this passage. I do not comprehend just how awesome He is. His holiness, righteousness, and ultimate maturity are shown to everyone, not just to those who love Him. His goodness is shown to those who even oppose Him. So keep on asking, seeking, and knocking for them as well in order to be like the Father.

Jesus wants me to treat others with the same regard as I would my son or me. This is a little deeper than my plow goes down. I guess it is a matter of maturity. If God does, then I am called to be like Him. As a matter of fact, John 3:16 goes even further. God loved me even more than His own Son. Now, that is a call to maturity. You see, there is a big difference between selfishness and selflessness. It is the place to which God is trying to get us. It is the sum of what He wants His creation to be. It is the difference between pride and humility. Pride breeds selfishness. Humility fosters selflessness. Here I have to go back to the beginning of the beginning. "Poor in spirit" is still involved even as Jesus begins to conclude His sermon. I pray that I can learn this lesson. Lord, help me to be selfless.

TWENTY-FOUR

The Path of Least Resistance–
Attitude toward Responsibility

Enter through the narrow gate. For wide is the gate
and broad is the road that leads to destruction,
and many enter through it. But small is the gate
and narrow the road that leads to life, and only a
few find it.
–MATTHEW 7:13–14

am so glad that life is not determined by a poll. I am glad that God does not take a poll and then decide based on what everybody thinks. Many think that the majority of people are the determining factor as to what is right and wrong. The majority of opinion polls have become the standard for many news networks (unless they disagree with the opinion). It is unfortunate that polls of opinions have become the means for determining laws in our nation. I heard a man say the other day, "For God so loved the world that He didn't take a poll."

This is the heart of this section. It deals with two different perspectives. It is the easy versus the difficult. It is the attitude toward responsibility and consequences. Jesus knows my nature. He knows that what I want is usually determined by what is easiest. He knows that what is easier demands less responsibility and, maybe, more consequences. That is the underlying attitude involved in this section.

He begins with two gates, two roads, and travelers. The gates are defined as being one wide and one narrow. The roads are defined as wide and narrow as well. The gate and the road that are wide lead to destruction. The gate and the road that are narrow lead to life. The result is that many choose the wide and few choose the narrow.

The reason that many are on the wide road is that it requires no effort. The wide gate is passed through with no particular purpose in mind. It is the aimless way. The road is the same. I can travel on this road unconsciously. It requires nothing more than what I want. That is a popular choice because many are on that road. It is the majority. It requires no searching. This road has unlimited access and has no apparent boundaries. The consequences of traveling on this road and passing through this gate are that they lead to destruction.

The small gate and the narrow road require something

altogether different. Traveling down this path is a conscious effort. It requires searching. It requires discipline. It is not a popular choice by any stretch of the imagination. The gate has extremely limited access. The road has defined and limited boundaries. It requires the responsibility of the traveler. The consequence of travel on this road is life.

This is the beginning of the conclusion. Jesus begins to ask for a choice. This choice is not the choice of the majority. It is the choice of the few. The implication of this section is, the wide gate and wide road represent those who choose not to follow Jesus's teaching. The narrow gate and narrow road represent those who do follow Jesus's teaching. Jesus is making a difference between two things. The comparison is between the Jews' teachings and Jesus's teachings. The comparison is not between the law and Jesus's teachings. This is important to understand. It is what the Jews taught about the law. What the Jews taught was much easier. It was manipulated to suit their purposes. It was easy and mindless. Jesus's teaching, on the other hand, necessitated discipline and thought.

Jesus is saying that destruction comes from not following His teachings. Following Jesus is a conscious, disciplined decision. It is a choice. It is not a haphazard majority-rule way of life. The majority rule is not the standard unless the majority is following Jesus's standard. Henry David Thoreau said, "The path of least resistance leads to crooked rivers and crooked men."[16] It is easy not to follow Jesus. To follow Him requires discipline. The majority is easy. The minority is disciplined. The majority enter the world gate. The minority enters the life gate.

This is the point of the whole section. Each one will take

---

[16]   Thoreau, Henry David. QuoteTab.com. www.quotetab.com/quote/by-henry-david-thoreau/the-path-of-least-resistance-leads-to-crooked-rivers-and-crooked-men?source=men., 2022.

responsibility for the choices that are made on the road. Each one will accept the consequences for the choices they make. It is not determined by what happened to me as a child. It is a matter of my conscious choice now. Which am I willing to choose? Am I willing to choose to follow Jesus down a path that is less traveled? Am I willing to choose to follow Him down the road that requires discipline? Am I willing to submit my will to His will in the matter? If I choose to follow, then I will gain life. Life is the consequence of following Jesus. It is my responsibility to choose which road I will travel. If I choose not to follow Him, then I am responsible for that choice as well. The consequence of that choice is destruction. I pray that I choose responsibly. I pray that I will not follow the course of least resistance. Oh, it is easier, but the end is destruction. It takes meekness to follow Jesus. It takes discipline and control. I wonder what a poll of registered voters would say about the wide gate and the narrow gate. Lord, help me to follow you.

TWENTY-FIVE

Wolves and Fruit–
Attitude toward God's Will

Watch out for false prophets. They come to you in sheep's clothing, but inwardly they are ferocious wolves. By their fruit you will recognize them. Do people pick grapes from thorn bushes, or figs from thistles? Likewise, every good tree bears good fruit, but a bad tree bears bad fruit. A good tree cannot bear bad fruit, and a bad tree cannot bear good fruit. Every tree that does not bear good fruit is cut down and thrown into the fire. Thus, by their fruit you will recognize them. Not everyone who says to me, "Lord, Lord," will enter the kingdom of heaven, but only he who does the will of my Father who is in heaven. Many will say to me on that day, "Lord, Lord, did we not prophesy in your name, and in your name drive out demons and perform many miracles?" Then I will tell them plainly, "I never knew you. Away from me, you evildoers!"
–MATTHEW 7:15–23

n an ideal world, there would be no one to deceive. In an ideal world, there would be no one with ulterior motives. In an ideal world, life would reflect truth. Unfortunately, this is not an ideal world. The influence of the evil one has taken its toll on just about everything. The influence of evil, however unspeakable, has taken its toll on religious teachers. The same was true in the first century. The dark side influenced the teachers of law and the scribes. Some who even followed Jesus were taken with ulterior motives. When evil tempts and overcomes those who believe, then their will becomes paramount. The will of the Father is not held in high esteem. It is rather used to manipulate others to follow personal wills.

As Jesus concludes His sermon, the tragedy of the reality of false teaching is exposed. False teachers are more concerned with their personal gain than with the will of the Father. When I mean personal gain, I am not just talking about money. Of course, money is always a motive for changing to manipulate but there are other things that can become personal gain. Personal gain can be influence, pride-filled attitudes, or anything that can be used to enhance the position of the teacher.

All these things are reasons that are used so that the ulterior motives of the teacher can deceive. But the ultimate thing that the deliberate misuse of God's word indicates is a lack of respect for the will of God. That is why the bottom-line attitude of this section is the attitude toward God's will. If God's will is held in high esteem, then God is held in high esteem. If God's will is not held in honor, then the indication is that God is not held in honor.

Jesus warns that there are false prophets. That is the reality of the real world. They are disguised. They look different from what they really are. The outward perception reflects good, honorable people. But the inward part is anything but good and honorable. Jesus compares these disguised teachers to wolves in sheep's clothing. The false teachers look, smell, and even feel like sheep. Yet they are simply wolves that look, smell, and feel like sheep. The whole purpose of being perceived as sheep is to cloak the fact they are wolves. They act like wolves. Sheep never leave wolf tracks. That is the key. False teachers can be exposed. They are exposed by the lives they live. The fruit they bear exposes them.

Jesus says that there is a contrast between their teaching and their lives. The fruit they bear is the flaw in the costume. The fruit is the indicator. Jesus makes this identity a matter of recognition. He uses the illustration of grapes and figs. Grapes come from grape vines. Figs come from fig trees. I cannot get grapes from thornbushes. I cannot get figs from thistles. The tree produces its own kind. Good trees do not produce bad fruit. Bad trees do not produce good fruit. It is by the fruit of their lives that a false teacher is recognized. The fruit from the tree exposes the disguise. No matter what the tree looks like, the fruit will expose it for what it is. I do not have the ability or the skill to determine a false teacher by any other means.

God, on the other hand, can. He can look into the heart. He knows the truth. He knows the actions. He knows the motives. That is why Jesus says that entering the kingdom is not a matter of mere words. It is not a matter of speech. He says it is a matter of action. That action is doing the will of the Father. His words are "Not everyone who says, 'Lord, Lord,' will enter the kingdom of heaven, but only he who does the will of my Father who is in heaven." It is a matter of action from the heart. As we have seen in the sermon, He desires the right thing done with the right motive. The Pharisees were doing the right things. They did good deeds, they prayed, and they fasted. All these things were right. These things were God's will. They were for the wrong purpose. The Pharisees had the wrong motives. So doing God's will with the right motives is what God wants.

Doing the will of the Father is the important thing. It is not the appearance of religion. The prophecy was right. Driving out demons was right. Performing miracles was right. Yet Jesus says that these things can be wrong to the extent that something was missing. What was missing was God.

The will of the Father is how I am known by Jesus. If I am more concerned with appearance than the will of the Father, then I am missing the point. Mere appearance only ends in separation. Jesus will see to that. He will say, "I never knew you. Away from me, you evildoers!" Jesus will make that call. That separation is the same thing as what will happen to the tree that does not bear good fruit. It will be cut down and thrown into the fire.

If there is a false teacher, then that implies that there is a true teacher. If there is a true teacher, then the implication is there is a standard of truth. If there is a standard of truth, then it can be deviated from. When the standard of truth is deviated from, then those who deviate from the standard are not true teachers. If one is not a true teacher, then, well, you fill in the blank. The will of the Father is the standard.

Jesus makes the implication that motives are crucial to the truth as well. He is the determining factor as to the motives. My role as a sheep is to make sure my motives and my actions follow God's will. My role as a sheep is to look at my life and ensure that my life reflects my role as a sheep.

There are basically three things that are key elements involved in following the will of the Father. They are truth, action, and motive. If truth is not important, then the will of the Father becomes unimportant to me. If I talk the talk but do not walk the walk, then the will of the Father is unimportant to me. If my motives are for my glory rather than God's glory, then the will of the Father is unimportant to me. My esteem for the will of the Father reflects my esteem for the Father. Jesus is calling for His disciples to cherish the Father's will in truth, action, and motive. Lord, help me to cherish.

TWENTY-SIX

The Wise Man Built ... –
Attitude toward Wisdom

Therefore everyone who hears these words of
mine and puts them into practice is like a wise
man who built his house on a rock. The rain came
down, the streams rose, and the winds blew against
that house; yet it did not fall, because it had its
foundation on the rock. But everyone who hears
these words of mine and does not put them into
practice is like a foolish man who built his house on
sand. The rain came down, the streams rose, and
the winds blew and beat against that house, and it
fell with a great crash.
–MATTHEW 7:24–27

Storms are a part of life. They come to everyone. Storms are not always wind and rain. They are not always snow and hail. They are not always floods. They *are* sometimes cancer. They are sometimes heart attacks. They are sometimes diseases that render a person useless. They may be in the form of persecution. They may be in the form of suffering. Storms come in a variety of sizes, shapes, and severity. The fact remains that storms do come. They even come to believers. That is the very thing that Jesus was trying to impress upon the Jews on the mount. These people were children of God. They believed in Him. Yet sometimes, even those who believed in Him showed evidence of storms. He could see it in the lines on their faces. He could see it in the color of their hair. He could see it in their countenance. He could see it in their eyes. They wanted to know how to weather the storm. Maybe they thought He would take all the storms away. Some still do. He did not come to take all the storms away. He came to keep the house standing when the storms passed. He came to give substance to life so that when the storms do come, I can still have peace.

This is another one of those "therefore" passages. It is a conclusion. It is *the* conclusion. This is what matters. So what is the "therefore" there for? It is there for what came before. This is why the sermon is so relevant today. Jesus is the focus of life. The evil one will try everything and anything to take the eyes and heart of the believer off the Master. It is the Master that keeps our focus crystal clear. It is the Master that gives the believer something solid to build on. Here it is again. It is a choice. Either I choose to build on Jesus or choose to build on me.

This is wisdom. That is what Jesus says. It is the wise one who chooses Jesus. It is the foolish one who chooses self. Jesus's ultimate conclusion deals with the attitude toward wisdom. This section is another comparison. It is the comparison between the wise and the foolish builders.

Jesus compares the man who hears His words and puts them into practice to a wise man who built his house upon a rock. This wise man found a solid foundation for his house. His house weathered the storm. The rain came down. The streams rose. The winds blew and beat against the house. It stood firm. It did not fall. The house was not the key. It was not the building materials. It was not the one who built it. It was the foundation that kept the house intact. The foolish man is the one who hears the words of Jesus and does not put them into practice. He built his house upon the sand. It did not weather the storm. The rain came down. The streams rose. The winds blew and beat against the house. It fell with a great crash because the foundation was not solid.

I was thinking of buying a house one time down on the coast of North Carolina. The place was Wilmington. During the previous few years, this area seemed to be a catcher's mitt for hurricanes. It seemed like every storm either hit like a fastball or curved to hit the mitt. There had been a lot of damage. They had adjusted the building codes so that new houses that were being built could withstand the winds and rains. The man who was trying to sell me the house had a real sales pitch. He knew that I was a minister, so he told me of his faith. I asked him what kind of foundation the house had been built on. He said it was the best foundation that there was. It was concrete poured over a bed of sand. I questioned, "Sand?" He said that it was considered the best foundation that money could buy. I said, "Is that why the Empire State Building was built on two hundred feet of bedrock?" I told him, "I read somewhere that a man built his house on the sand, and it fell. It did not fall when the weather was pretty. It fell when the storms came, and I understand that your storms around here are so bad that they even give them names." He embarrassedly said that they simply met the building codes. I passed on the house.

Jesus is not talking about building codes for greater Jerusalem.

He is talking about life. The house represents my life of faith. The storms represent the trials of life. The after-storm result is whether or not my faith remains intact. Remember, we are not talking about a gentle spring rain. It is not a breeze blowing through the trees, making the leaves rustle. It is a storm. It beats upon the house. It is powerful. It is dynamic. It can change everything. Storms can do one of two things. It can make me or break me. The foundation is the key to whether it makes me or breaks me.

This is the conclusion to the matter. Jesus did not come merely to change my actions. He came to change my attitude of the heart. When my attitudes are changed, then my actions will follow. If my attitudes are not changed, then the actions will not change either. Jesus puts it this way. If I hear his words and do not change my attitude, then I will not put His words into practice in my life. This attitude change is my attitude toward Jesus as opposed to my attitude toward me. I can hear all the words that Jesus spoke. I can be exposed to His teachings. If I do not change my attitude toward Him, then my actions will not follow Him. If I do not change my attitude, then I am still doing what I want rather than what He wants. The point is that if I do not follow Jesus's teachings, my life will end in disaster. If I do follow Jesus's teachings, then my life will flourish even in the storm.

The key to living in this world is Jesus. He is what makes the difference. If I, as a Christian, wring my hands when storms come into my life, what makes me any different from someone who does not have Jesus as their master? Storms come to everyone. The difference between the lives of those who follow Jesus and those who do not follow Him is not their lives but what, or rather, Who their lives are built upon. The sermon is the teaching that I can build my life on. The reason the sermon is so important is because it gives believers something to build on and maintain that relationship with God. It is the way to maturity. It is through this relationship with God and the maturity that comes with it that storms are weathered. The sermon bases my life on God, not the appearances to men. God is solid. He always has been. He always will be. He is the rock. Appearance is unstable. It always has been. It always will be. It is nothing more than sand that wind can blow, and rain can wash away.

When my life is based on God, then He is my foundation. He cannot be shaken or moved. If my life is built on Him, then my house cannot be shaken because He is my foundation. You understand that both the wise and the foolish builders were familiar with Jesus's teachings. Both had heard what He had to say. Jesus was talking to people who were covenant children of God. So Jesus is referring to two believers. He is not referring to a believer and someone who does not believe. "The wise and foolish" refers to two different people who profess faith in God. The difference between the two is the real foundation. Now the question comes to me and to you. Whom have I chosen? These words found in Matthew 5, 6, and 7 can form my heart, transform my mind, and conform my will. It is a choice. That is what makes you and me different from everything else in creation. When I choose Him, He is glorified. Wouldn't you like to pull back the curtain of heaven and take a peek at what happens when you choose God? Lord, help me to be wise.

AFTER THE FACT

> When Jesus had finished saying these things, the crowds were amazed at His teaching, because He taught as one who had authority, and not as their teachers of the law. (Matthew 7:28–29)

Jesus finished. The response was amazement. That is what I hope the response is today with His words. He taught like no one they ever heard. He taught like no one I should ever hear either. His words came with authority because He knew God and He knew man. He is the only one who can take the things of God and communicate them so effectively to the heart of man. He was the Son of the Creator and the son of a carpenter. He was God and man. He took common things and transformed them into concepts of deity.

Simple things like salt, light, anger, hatred, hands, eyes, yes, no, cheeks, cloaks, sunshine, and rain are elevated to holy realms of illustration. Giving to the needy, prayer, fasting, treasures, lilies, birds, sawdust, and wood are used to communicate God's truths. Gifts, gates, fruit, thorns, rock, and sand are plain things. But put all these things on the lips of the Master, and He can transform them into pictures of truth that can change, mold, and mature even hard-hearted, stiff-backed Jews. The good news is that they can still change, mold, and mature people like you and me too.

He has called for His people to make a decision. This decision is not for the purpose of hindering or burdening His disciple. It is for the purpose of moving His disciple to a mature relationship with the Father. As the relationship matures, the load becomes lighter and the burden easier. It is not because of us but because of Him. When I move into a more mature relationship with God where perception is not the issue, but God's glory is, then when the storms come and beat on my house, my faith will continue in Him, and my house will stand. My foundation will not wash away. My rock will not be blown over, so my house will stay intact.

May the Lord of Creation and carpenters use His words in His sermon to move us to a higher level of maturity and a deeper relationship with Him. Thank you for sharing this trip with me. May our hearts be softened and then molded to conform to His image. The Sermon on the Mount is a mountain of a sermon. The Sermon on the Mount compared to all the sermons that I have ever preached or heard is like comparing Mt. Everest to an anthill. So keep on reading His sermon. Keep on reading Matthew 5–7. The Lord is the one who will do our reforming, transforming, and conforming. May the Lord bless you in your maturity.

THINGS TO CONSIDER– SURPASSING RIGHTEOUSNESS

What is the difference between the righteousness of the Pharisees and the teachers of the law and the righteousness that *surpasses* the righteousness of the Pharisees and the teachers of the law?

It Could Be a Couple of Things
Matthew 5:17–20

1. In view of verse 17 "Do not think that I have come to abolish the Law or the Prophets; I have not come to abolish them but to fulfill them."
2. In view of verse 18 "Until heaven and earth disappear, not the smallest letter, not the least stroke of a pen, will by any means disappear from the law until everything is accomplished."
3. In view of verse 19 "Anyone who breaks one of the least of these commands and teaches others to do the same."

When Do These Things Happen?

I have not come to abolish them but to fulfill them
… Not the smallest letter, not the least stroke of a

pen, will by any means disappear from the law until everything is accomplished. (Matthew 5:17–18)

For what the law was powerless to do because it was weakened by the flesh, God did by sending His own Son in the likeness of sinful flesh to be a sin offering. And so he condemned sin in the flesh, in order that the righteous requirements of the law might be fully met in us, who do not live according to the sinful nature but according to the Spirit. (Romans 8:3–4)

Yet he did not waver through unbelief regarding the promise of God but was strengthened in his faith and gave glory to God, being fully persuaded that God had power to do what he had promised. This is why "it was credited to him" as righteousness. (Romans 4:20–22) @ Abram (Genesis 15:6)

The words "it was credited to him" were written not for him alone, but also for us, to whom God will credit righteousness—for us who believe in Him who raised Jesus our Lord from the dead. (Romans 4:23–24)

So What Is Surpassing Righteousness?

God made Him who had no sin to be sin for us, so that in Him we might become the righteousness of God. (2 Corinthians 5:21)

Could It Be?

In Matthew 5:20, Jesus was talking about us receiving God's righteousness and Jesus taking our sin when He said, "For I tell you that unless your righteousness surpasses that of the Pharisees and the teachers of the law, you will certainly not enter the kingdom of heaven."

It could be that when Jesus "fulfilled them" and "everything was accomplished," He took our sin, and we were credited with the surpassing righteousness of God.

And don't you think that
His righteousness *is surpassing*? (Romans 8:3-4 and 2 Corinthians 5:21)

ADDENDUM

In Romans 9 and 10, Paul explains the righteousness of God, which I believe to be the real surpassing righteousness. This may be what Jesus was probably speaking of when He taught in Matthew 5:20, "For I tell you that unless your righteousness surpasses that of the Pharisees and the teachers of the law, you will certainly not enter the kingdom of heaven."

So what is the righteousness that surpasses that of the Pharisees and teachers of the law?

Romans 9:30–33 begins my endeavor to explain the righteousness that surpasses that of the Pharisees and the teachers of the law.

> What then shall we say? That the Gentiles, who did not pursue righteousness, have obtained it, a righteousness that is by faith; but the people of Israel, who pursued the law as the way of righteousness, have not attained their goal. Why not? Because they pursued it not by faith but as if it were by works. They stumbled over the stumbling stone. As it is written: "See, I lay in Zion a stone that causes people to stumble and a rock that makes them fall, and the one who believes in him will never be put to shame." (Isaiah 8:14, 28:16)

Then follows Romans 10:1–4:

> Brothers and sisters, my heart's desire and prayer to God for the Israelites is that they may be saved. For I can testify about them that they are zealous for God, but their zeal is not based on knowledge. Since they did not know the righteousness of God *and sought to establish their own*, they did not submit to God's righteousness. Christ is the culmination of the law so that there may be righteousness for everyone who believes.

This seemed to be my problem: *I sought to establish my own righteousness.* This righteousness is no better than the righteousness of the Pharisees and the teachers of the law, no matter what law it is. When I try to do as they do, I become like them. My rightness is only for others to see. I tend to believe that I can do the things that please and fulfill what the Lord wants. Jesus becomes no more than a spare tire for me. I believe I am doing all the things God wants. Then, I realized that I may have missed something and went flat. Only then do I call on Jesus to repair me again. He will make me new again. Off I go, forgiven and in good standing again. So I go back to establishing my own rightness just where I left off.

There are also times I do what I do not want to do (Romans 7:19). How do I rectify that? Can I do enough of my own rightness to make up for the things I did not want to do? Of course, the answer is no. Back to Jesus, my spare tire. I cry out, "Fix me, fix me, please fix me." All the while, I depend on myself to do right, to establish my own righteousness.

Obviously, Galatians 2:21, "I do not set aside the Grace of God, for if righteousness could be gained through the law, Christ died for nothing!" describes my problem.

Again, in Galatians 3:21 (Is the law, therefore, opposed to the promises of God? Absolutely not! For if a law had been given that could impart life, then righteousness would certainly have come by the law) there is a problem. This surpassing righteousness does not come by law, any law. This righteousness only comes by faith in Jesus.

As we go through the Gospels and Acts, we find that Romans speak a little more in-depth about righteousness, the righteousness that we have. It is a righteousness that comes by faith that is like the righteousness that Abraham had: "Abraham believed God, and it was credited to him as righteousness" (Genesis 15:6, Romans 4:21–22). Faith has always been dovetailed with righteousness for God's covenant people: "The righteous will live by faith" (Habakkuk 2:4). Paul outlined Abraham's faith in Romans 4:17–22 by writing three things that He believed (his faith):

1. He believed God could give life to the dead,
2. He believed God could call things that are not as though they were (NIV 1984), and
3. He believed God had the power to do what He had promised.

We also believe God when He promised to bring us from death to eternal life by the power of Jesus's sacrifice on the cross. We also believe God can call things that are not as though they were. We also believe God has the power to do what He promises. This is one way God credits us with righteousness. Now we are not righteous in and of ourselves. Jesus was not sin in and of Himself. But "God made Him who had no sin to be sin for us, so that in Him we might become the righteousness of God" (2 Corinthians 5:21). That is how God credits us with righteousness. When we were raised from death to life (Romans 6:1–4):

What shall we say, then? Shall we go on sinning so that grace may increase? By no means! We are those who have died to sin; how can we live in it any longer? Or don't you know that all of us who were baptized into Christ Jesus were baptized into his death? We were therefore buried with him through baptism into death in order that, just as Christ was raised from the dead through the glory of the Father, we too may live a new life.

He also said in verse 13 of the same chapter, "Do not offer any part of yourself to sin as an instrument of wickedness, but rather offer yourselves to God as those who have been brought from death to life; and offer every part of yourself to him as an instrument of righteousness." So we believe God as Abraham did that:

1. He believed God could give life to the dead. (We do too because we believe that we have been brought from spiritual death to spiritual life.)
2. He believed God could call things that are not as though they were. (We do too because we believe that we have been credited with righteousness and Jesus was counted as sin on our behalf.)
3. He believed God had the power to do what He had promised. (We do too because we believe God has the power to do what He promised. He can forgive us because Jesus (being sinless) suffered the wrath of God for our sins.)

If someone else thinks they have reasons to put confidence in the flesh, I have more: circumcised on the eighth day of the people of Israel, of the tribe of Benjamin, a Hebrew of Hebrews; in regard to the law, a Pharisee; as for zeal, persecuting the church; as for righteousness based on the law, faultless. But whatever were gains to me I now consider loss for the sake of Christ. What is more, I consider everything a loss because of the surpassing worth of knowing Christ Jesus my Lord, for whose sake I have lost all things. I consider them garbage, that I may gain Christ and be found in him, not having a righteousness of my own that comes from the law, but that which is through Faith in Christ—the righteousness that comes from God on the basis of faith. (Philippians 3:4–9)

But now a righteousness of God, apart from law, has been made known, to which the Law and the Prophets testify. This righteousness comes through Faith in Jesus Christ to all who believe. (Romans 3:21–22)

The words "it was credited to him" were written not for him alone, but also for us, to whom God will credit righteousness—for us who believe in him who raised Jesus our Lord from the dead. (Romans 4:23–24)

Here is a question of concern for me and maybe for you. I do not live righteously. Oh, I suppose there are times that I do, but that righteousness is like what Isaiah and Paul said about their righteousness. It is like the righteousness that Jesus said about the Pharisees. So do I need the sacrifice of the blood of Jesus just when I do not live righteously? Or am I OK with God in between the sins?

Paul said this in Philippians 3:4–9:

If someone else thinks they have reasons to put confidence in the flesh, I have more: circumcised on the eighth day, of the people of Israel, of the tribe of Benjamin, a Hebrew of Hebrews; in regard to the law, a Pharisee; as for zeal, persecuting the church; as for righteousness based on the law, faultless.But whatever were gains to me I now consider loss for the sake of Christ. What is more, I consider everything a loss because of the surpassing worth of knowing Christ Jesus my Lord, for whose sake I have lost all things. I consider them garbage that I may gain Christ and be found in him, not having a righteousness of my own that comes from the law, but that which is through Faith in Christ—the righteousness that comes from God on the basis of faith.

The word for *garbage* can also be translated as rubbish, any refuse as the excrement of animals, offscouring, rubbish, dregs, etc. (Authorized Version—dung), i.e., worthless and detestable.[17]

All of us have become like one who is unclean, and all our righteous acts are like filthy rags; we

---

[17]	Greek–English Lexicon of the New Testament, Grimm's Wilke's Clavis Novi Testament, Translated Revised and Enlarged by Joseph Henry Thayer, D. D., Late Bussey Professor of New Testament Criticism and Interpretation in the Divinity School of Harvard University. Zondervan Publishing House of the Zondervan Corporation, Grand Rapids, Michigan 49506, Seventeenth Zondervan printing 1976] page 580-B. All Rights Reserved.

all shrivel up like a leaf, and like the wind our sins sweep us away. (Isaiah 64:6 NIV)

But we are all as an unclean thing, and all our righteousness are as filthy rags; and we all do fade as a leaf; and our iniquities, like the wind, have taken us away. (Isaiah 64:6 KJV)

Henry Neufeld says, "But today in reading Isaiah 64 in several translations I came across Isaiah 64:6 (5 in Hebrew) in which the phrase 'all our righteousness are as filthy rags' (KJV) occurs. Now having just read this in Hebrew I was reminded that the literal translation of this is 'menstrual cloths' or something similar. These cloths would be unclean, as was the woman in her menstrual period. One extended discussion of the issue of uncleanness can be found in Leviticus 15:19–33."[18]

I am not ashamed of the gospel because it is the power of God for the salvation of everyone who believes: first for the Jew, then for the Gentile. For in the gospel a righteousness from God is revealed, a righteousness that is by faith from first to last, just as it is written: "The righteous will live by faith." [Habakkuk 2:4] (Romans 1:16–17)

But now a righteousness of God, apart from law, has been made known, to which the Law and the Prophets testify. This righteousness comes through Faith in Jesus Christ to all who believe. (Romans 3:21–22)

---

18 https://henryneufeld.com/threads/2007/03/29/isaiah-646-menstrual-cloth

What then shall we say that Abraham, our forefather according to the flesh, discovered in this matter? If, in fact, Abraham was justified by works, he had something to boast about—but not before God. What does scripture say? "Abraham believed God, and it was credited to him as righteousness." (Romans 4:1–3)

As it is written, "I have made you a father of many nations." He is our father in the sight of God, in whom he believed—the God who gives life to the dead and calls into being things that were not. Against all hope, Abraham in hope believed and so became the father of many nations, just as it had been said to him, "So shall your offspring be." Without weakening in his faith, he faced the fact that his body was as good as dead—since he was about a hundred years old—and that Sarah's womb was also dead. Yet he did not waver through unbelief regarding the promise of God but was strengthened in his faith and gave glory to God, being fully persuaded that God had power to do what he had promised. This is why "it was credited to him as righteousness." The words "it was credited to him" were written not for him alone, but also for us, to whom God will credit righteousness—for us who believe in him who raised Jesus our Lord from the dead. He was delivered over to death for our sins and was raised to life for our justification. (Romans 4:17–25)

Unfortunately for me, or should I say, "Blessed am I," I am in need of Jesus even in between the sins! When I thought I was establishing my own righteousness in between my sins, I found out my righteousness is nothing but refuse, garbage, dung, or any other worthless or detestable thing. I need Jesus's righteousness in between, before and after my sins. When I walk in the light (1 John 1:5–10), then His blood keeps on cleansing me. That is how unrighteous me has fellowship with holy, holy, holy God and Father and with His holy, holy, holy Son, Lord, Anointed One, Jesus, and God. There is absolutely no comparison between my righteousness and the Holy One of Israel. Jesus took the punishment of the wrath of God for my sin on the cross and by faith the Father credits me with His righteousness (Isaiah 53:1–11, 2 Corinthians 5:19–21).

BIBLIOGRAPHY

1. Barclay, William. *And Jesus Said: A Handbook on the Parables of Jesus.* Philadelphia, Pennsylvania: The Westminster Press, 1970.
2. Cope, Mike. *Righteousness Inside Out.* Nashville, Tennessee: Christian Communications, a division of the Gospel Advocate Co., 1988.
3. Edersheim, Alfred. *The Temple: Its Ministry and Services (Updated Edition).* Peabody, Massachusetts: Hendrickson Publishers Inc., 1994.
4. Kell, Frank Ted. *Sermon on the Mount* (Class Notes). Lubbock, Texas: Sunset School of Preaching, 1978.
5. Jones, Dr. Jerry. *Beyond the Storm: Finding God's Calm Assurance.* West Monroe, Louisiana: Howard Publishing Company, Inc., 1997.
6. LaHaye, Tim. *The Battle for the Mind.* Old Tappan, New Jersey: Flemming H. Revell Co., 1980.
7. McGuiggan, Jim. *The Reign of God.* Lubbock, Texas: Montex Publishing Company, 1979.
8. McGuiggan, Jim. *Life on the Ash Heap: Job Fights God's Battle for Him.* Webb City, Missouri: Covenant Publishing, 2003.
9. Neufeld, Henry. Isaiah 64:6 Menstrual Cloth. TNIV. Blog, 2007.
10. Peretti, Frank. *Focus on the Family.* Radio Broadcast, 1980-1989.

11. Scripture taken from the Holy Bible, New International Version (NIV) © 1973, 1978, 1984, by International Bible Society. Used by permission of Zondervan Publishing House. All rights reserved.

12. Thoreau, Henry David. QuoteTab.com. www.quotetab.com/quote/by-henry-david-thoreau/the-path-of-least-resistance-leads-to-crooked-rivers-and-crooked-men?source=men., 2022.

ABOUT THE AUTHOR

Kim resides in his family's homeplace in the rural Appalachian Mountains of West Virginia. He has been married to his high school sweetheart, Brenda, for 50 years and they have two children and five grandchildren. Kim attended Sunset School of Preaching, in Lubbock, Texas, and graduated in 1979. In 2009, he earned a Bachelor of Biblical Studies Degree from Sunset International Bible Institute. He has been a minister for forty-four years, spreading the word of God to many.

Printed in the USA
CPSIA information can be obtained
at www.ICGtesting.com
CBHW020604150824
13134CB00009B/148/J

9 798385 015948